'*Be The Jellyfish Training Manual* is a delight; a comprehensive and fun-filled guide for any adult wishing to support the emotional and social well-being of children. Packed with ideas and easy-to-access plans and resources, it will pre-empt many of the questions adults may feel when approaching this vital aspect of learning whilst also recognising the importance of nurturing creativity in the classroom.'

– Sandra Hooper and Mary Atkinson, co-founders of Story Massage

BE THE JELLYFISH TRAINING MANUAL

of related interest

Sitting on a Chicken
The Best (Ever) 52 Yoga Games to Teach in Schools
Michael Chissick
Illustrated by Sarah Peacock
ISBN 978 1 84819 325 3
eISBN 978 0 85701 280 7

More Creative Coping Skills for Children
Activities, Games, Stories, and Handouts to Help Children Self-regulate
Bonnie Thomas
ISBN 978 1 78592 021 9
eISBN 978 1 78450 267 6

Once Upon a Touch…
Story Massage for Children
Mary Atkinson and Sandra Hooper
ISBN 978 1 84819 287 4
eISBN 978 0 85701 234 0

Focusing and Calming Games for Children
Mindfulness Strategies and Activities to Help Children to Relax, Concentrate and Take Control
Deborah M. Plummer
Illustrated by Jane Serrurier
ISBN 978 1 84905 143 9
eISBN 978 0 85700 344 7

BE THE JELLYFISH

Training Manual

SUPPORTING CHILDREN'S SOCIAL AND EMOTIONAL WELLBEING

LUCY CREE AND SARAH BROGDEN

Jessica Kingsley *Publishers*
London and Philadelphia

First published in 2017
by Jessica Kingsley Publishers
73 Collier Street
London N1 9BE, UK
and
400 Market Street, Suite 400
Philadelphia, PA 19106, USA

www.jkp.com

Library of Congress Cataloging in Publication Data
Names: Cree, Lucy, author. | Brogden, Sarah, author.
Title: Be the Jellyfish training manual : supporting children's social and emotional wellbeing / Lucy Cree and Sarah Brogden.
Description: London : Jessica Kingsley Publishers, 2017.
Identifiers: LCCN 2016038365 (print) | LCCN 2016057715 (ebook) | ISBN 9781785922428 (alk. paper) | ISBN 9781784505226 (ebook)
Subjects: LCSH: Social learning--Great Britain--Handbooks, manuals, etc. | Affective education--Great Britain--Handbooks, manuals, etc.
Classification: LCC LC192.4 .C74 2017 (print) | LCC LC192.4 (ebook) | DDC 303.3/2--dc23

British Library Cataloguing in Publication Data
A CIP catalogue record for this book is available from the British Library

ISBN 978 1 78592 242 8
eISBN 978 1 78450 522 6

Printed and bound in Great Britain

MIX
Paper from responsible sources
FSC www.fsc.org FSC® C016379

To all our loved ones, who have bestowed upon us insightful advice, support, reassurance, time and copious amounts of tea from the beginning. Without you we would not have reached this stage in our Be the Jellyfish journey and are eternally grateful.

Contents

PERMISSION IS GIVEN TO PHOTOCOPY
ANY MARKED PAGES WITH A *

Disclaimer

Be the Jellyfish Ltd aims to support the social and emotional wellbeing of children through encouraging and facilitating opportunities for self-expression, relaxation and creativity.

This book is not intended as a substitute for the proper advice of medical or professional advisers, who should, as appropriate, be consulted with respect to any matter, symptom or condition that may require diagnosis or medical attention.

None of the Be the Jellyfish Ltd directors, officers, staff, consultants or teachers claim to be therapists or counsellors. They do not offer professional medical advice. They cannot advise on existing diagnosed problems. They cannot diagnose conditions, medical or otherwise. They cannot take responsibility for your own personal health or wellbeing. They do not heal or claim to heal participants of any physical or mental medical problems.

Be the Jellyfish Ltd excludes and disclaims all liability to any third party anywhere in the world for any injury, damage, direct or indirect loss, consequential or economic loss or any other loss, disruption or damage suffered as a result of the use of or reliance upon the information contained in this book, whether arising from omissions, negligence or otherwise to the maximum extent permitted by law.

Preface

Be the Jellyfish was created in 2014 by experienced primary school teachers to support the social and emotional wellbeing of children.

Jellyfish classes complement the work already undertaken in schools and the wider community and have proved successful in helping pupils to overcome behavioural difficulties and barriers to learning. They enable, facilitate and encourage self-expression, creativity and relaxation.

Our vision

Our vision is to support the social and emotional wellbeing of children through facilitating and encouraging self-expression, creativity and relaxation.

Mission statement

Our mission is to support adults in nurturing the social and emotional wellbeing of children.

Be the Jellyfish is delighted that you have chosen to join us in promoting and supporting social and emotional wellbeing.

With warmest wishes,

Lucy Cree and Sarah Brogden
Co-founders of Be the Jellyfish

Chapter 1

BE THE JELLYFISH AND JELLYFISH CLASSES

What does it mean to 'be the jellyfish'?

To 'be the jellyfish' is to experience a sense of calm, creativity and wellbeing. It is to be in the moment, to explore and express emotions safely and to recognize and be accepting of who we are.

This book provides adults with the information required to teach children how to 'be the jellyfish' through Jellyfish classes.

Aims of Jellyfish classes

Our aims are based on the **Jellyfish strands** and seek to support children to:

- **Discover** more about themselves, their relationships and the world around them
- **Explore** what they have discovered and gain a greater understanding and appreciation of themselves and who they are
- **Express** the possibilities of their imagination, their thoughts and their feelings
- **Manage** and acknowledge thoughts, feelings and situations using a range of tools and techniques
- **Develop** social and emotional growth so that they can move forward and make changes for the better

Benefits of Jellyfish classes

Jellyfish classes:

- Provide transferable skills and techniques for different situations, environments and future stresses
- Develop social communication skills and empathy
- Provide a positive outlet for feelings and emotions
- Improve confidence and self-esteem
- Support the removal of social, emotional and behavioural barriers to learning
- Improve challenging behaviour
- Develop a greater understanding of self
- Encourage self-expression
- Build resilience
- Instil a sense of calm and facilitate relaxation
- Improve feelings of stress, anxiety or nervousness
- Improve relationships and reduce bullying
- Add to an existing culture of care and wellbeing

All children can be invited to join and benefit from Jellyfish classes so that they have an opportunity to be creative, learn new techniques and experience a sense of calm and wellbeing.

Children with specific needs

Some children are in more need than others and therefore timetabled sessions within the school day are more suitable.

When identifying these children consider those displaying these common signs on a regular basis:

- Tummy aches/other persistent complaints
- Poor academic progress

- Nightmares/poor sleeping pattern
- Bed wetting/frequent use of bathroom
- Clingy/teary
- Low mood
- Hyper or inappropriate behaviour
- Difficulty communicating with adults or other children
- Elective mute
- Outbursts of anger, frustration and aggression
- Increased or loss of appetite
- Engaging in classroom avoidance tactics
- Indecisiveness
- Friendship difficulties
- Withdrawn

Implementing Jellyfish classes

There are many ways in which Jellyfish classes can be used with children.

Some suggestions to consider include:

- One-to-one mentoring
- Small focus and or intervention groups
- Whole class
- Mixed age group
- After-school class
- Parent and child class

When working with a large group or one with specific needs, it may be necessary to have at least two adults present so that children receive the maximum benefit of the classes.

Chapter 2

PREPARING FOR A JELLYFISH CLASS

The space

The environment should be prepared so that from the moment children enter a Jellyfish class the room is inviting and has a sense of calm. This communicates the tone of the class.

Ideally, shoes should be removed before the class begins and stored away from the activity areas. Children are also encouraged to wear comfortable clothing and bring along a cushion for any floor work.

Depending on the size of the group, classes can be held anywhere within a building so long as the space is contained and unlikely to be disturbed. This will help to create a feeling of safety and trust.

When working with an individual child or small group, a designated work room is useful; this can be set up on a smaller scale. For a large group a hall is ideal.

It is important that the room is prepared prior to the session. The table set up should be altered to suit the class and floor space available. This will enable children to see the room as a Jellyfish space.

Music

Music is key to creating the preferred atmosphere. There is no right or wrong when it comes to music selection so long as the piece is conducive to the mood that you wish to create. However, we would suggest that you do not use any music that contains lyrics (this excludes the music themed lesson) and would suggest classical or any music specifically designed for relaxation and meditation.

Music provides a gentle background noise from the moment children enter the room right up until the class has ended. Of course, there may be moments where you feel it is necessary to stop the music, for instance during a visualization or beginning a task. You are encouraged to use your professional judgement and be aware of the mood of the child, group or class you are working with.

Lighting

Like music, lighting is essential for creating the right atmosphere. Make every effort to block out natural light, as classes begin with minimal lighting in order to draw attention to the **focus point** in the centre of the room. Main lighting may be resumed to indicate to the children that they will be beginning their **creative expression** work.

Lighting is also recommended for use in the **sensory and relaxation zone**.

ROOM SET UP FOR A LARGE CLASS/GROUP

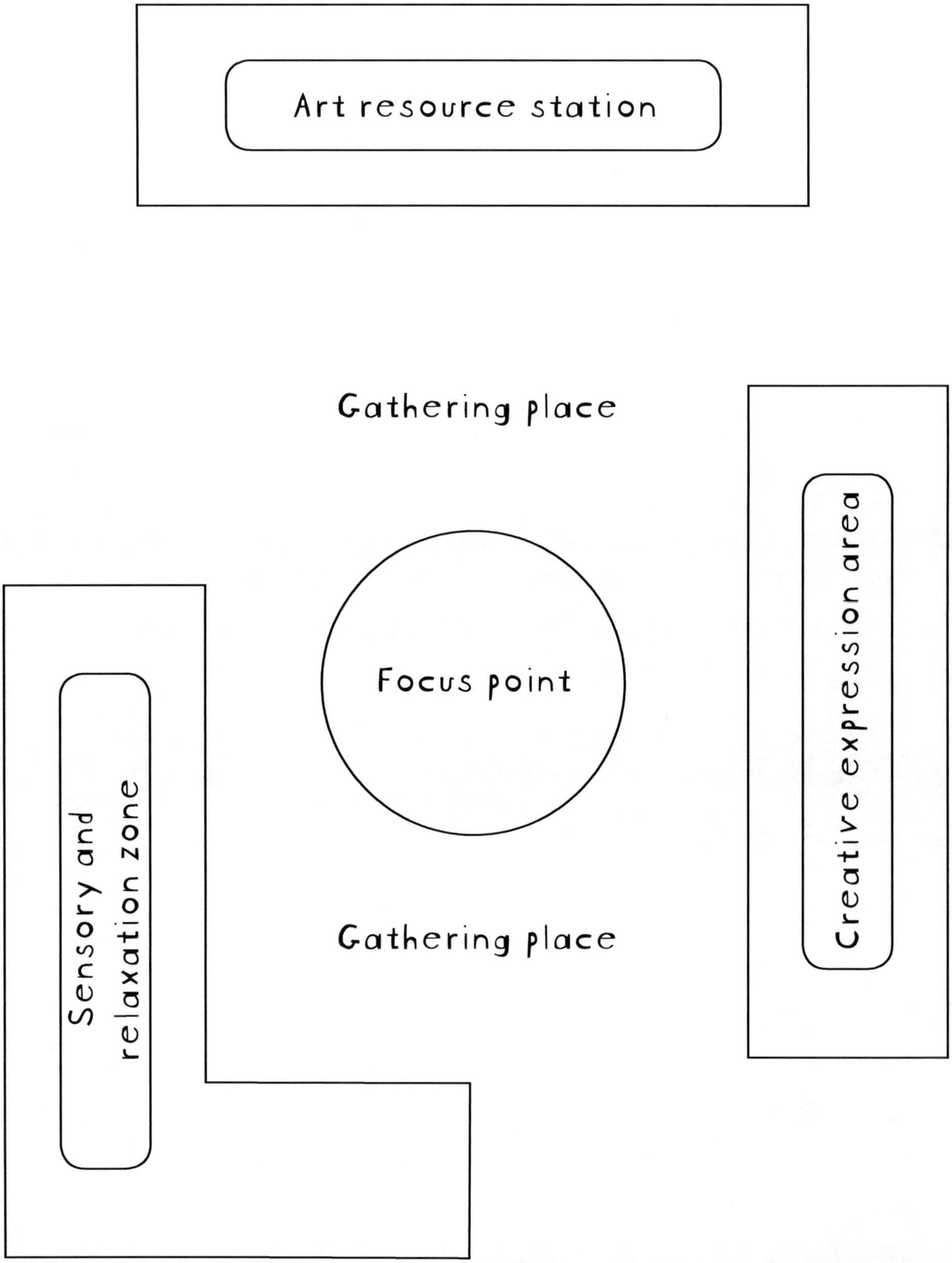

Gathering place

The **gathering place** is the most important area of the room, as this houses the **focus point** where the children meet and classes begin. Ideally, this should be in the centre of the room and the children should be taught to form a circle around it at the start of every class. The **focus point** should always have some form of lighting, which could be jellyfish themed but this is not essential, and be raised above floor level; an upturned box or small table is ideal for this. Other items and drapes should be added to the **focus point**, depending on the theme of the class.

Focus point suggestions

Block 1

Theme	Focus point suggestions
Jellyfish	A jellyfish tank, blue fabric
Elements	A rock, a candle, sand
Music	Images of music notes, instruments
Treasure	A decorative box, some coins, beads
Fantasy	A dragon, a shield, myth and legend books

Block 2

Theme	Focus point suggestions
Colour	A colour wheel, fabrics in different colours, a rainbow
Special Places	An empty frame, images of places – real or fictitious
Dreams	A dream catcher, clouds, a night light
Magic	A potion bottle, a wand, some glittery stars
Characters	Emoticons, images or models of familiar characters

Block 3

Theme	Focus point suggestions
Animals	Plastic animals, paw prints, animal print fabrics
Deep Space	A black cloth, space images, a fibre-optic light
Weather	Weather symbols, an umbrella, extreme weather photographs
Secret Garden	Flowers, packets of seeds, a flowerpot
Mirrors and Masks	A mirror, a variety of masks, a velvet drape

Block 4

Theme	Focus point suggestions
Circus	Brightly coloured fabric, bunting, juggling balls
Deserts	Sand, a cactus, some dried wood
Hats and Headdresses	A collection of hats and headdresses
Pockets	A large pocket or small collection of pockets, needles and thread
Footprints	Footprint templates

Block 5

Theme	Focus point suggestions
Books	A variety of books
Hot Air Balloons	Helium balloons, images of hot air balloons, cloud shapes
Textures	A patchwork blanket, textured squares/shapes
Messages	Envelopes, postcards, a bottle with a message inside
Butterflies	Images or models of butterflies

Block 6

Theme	Focus point suggestions
Rocks	A variety of different rocks or one large rock
Jellyfish Flurry	A jellyfish tank, blue fabric, images of different jellyfish
Puppets	A marionette puppet, a variety of hand or finger puppets
Angels	White fabric, angel wings, an angel figurine
Inventions	A toolbox, light bulbs, wires, batteries

Art resource station

This is the store for all art and craft materials (see 'Basic kit for art resource station' below). It is necessary to have a waste bin and a bucket in this area; the bucket can be used for children to deposit their used brushes and glue spreaders. Children will need to be taught how to use this area correctly and be shown how to dispense paint, glue, glitter and other materials. Children should be encouraged to be independent in acquiring what they need.

Basic kit for art resource station

- Colouring pencils
- Crayons
- Drawing pencils
- Felt tip pens
- Glitter
- Glue
- Paint
- Paintbrushes
- Paint palettes
- Scissors
- Sticky tape
- White and coloured chalks
- White, black and coloured card and paper

Some themes will require specialist materials that will need to be acquired and prepared in advance.

Specialist resources and equipment for specific themes

Theme	**Art and craft materials**
Characters	Human templates
Deep Space	Air-drying clay
Magic	Bottles and jars
Mirrors and Masks	Blank masks
Treasure	Boxes
Pockets	Felt, needles, thread
Puppets	Wooden spoons, fabric, wool
Footprints	Dough, air-drying clay
Rocks	Air-drying clay
Textures	Dough, foil embossing sheets
Messages	Voice recorder
Inventions	Junk items such as cardboard boxes, paper cups, egg boxes, yogurt pots, bubble wrap, drinking straws and bottle tops

Creative expression area

When it is time for children to create or respond to the theme of the class, they should be invited to join the **creative expression area**. For each class this should be set up using either covered tables or floor mats. It can be helpful to have a combination of both.

You are encouraged to make your own judgement as to how and when children are invited to collect the resources they need. For some groups it may be necessary to send them individually or in small groups or to set up selected materials in the area prior to the class.

If children do not wish to create using the art materials, invite them to spend time in the **gathering place** or **sensory and relaxation zone**. Children are encouraged to make the decision for themselves and to go by what is right for them.

The time children spend in the **creative expression area** should be entirely up to them although there is opportunity for direction. Some children will finish pieces within minutes whereas others will use the entire time allocated and even then may not finish. If time allows there should be no limit on the amount of **creative expression** produced; children should be encouraged to take pride and care in their work.

As the **creative expression** leads to the end of the class, children are invited to share their work with the group and given the option to discuss it. Ideally, work should be displayed in the **gathering place**, but only if the child is happy for this to happen.

To add to an environment of mutual respect, if physically able, children should clear away their own tools and materials. They need to be taught how to do this and the importance of doing so.

Sensory and relaxation zone

This zone is intended for quiet time but can also be used for thinking, relaxing, calming down and time out. Ideally, the focus here would be a dark tent or sheltered area. Within this tent there should be a variety of tactile fabrics, cushions, sensory toys and lights. Additional floor covering, cushions and lighting can also be introduced to create a peaceful setting.

To complement this area, we would also suggest that you provide a table or floor covering with resources such as peer massage tools, dough, emotional literacy books, colouring sheets, marbles, feathers, a tray of sand, puppets and some small world figures for children to use and explore.

The **sensory and relaxation zone** proves popular with children who find it difficult to express themselves through artwork or may not yet feel ready to do so.

Working with individuals and small groups

When working in a smaller space, all of the above areas should be incorporated but on a smaller scale with resources handpicked to suit the theme of the class, i.e. limit the range of art and craft materials for **creative expression** and choose items for the **sensory and relaxation zone** that you think would best reflect the theme.

What will the children need?

Children will need to bring along a small cushion to sit on whilst in the **gathering place** and for any relaxation activities unless you provide these. Ideally, children should wear a painting shirt for **creative expression** or change into comfortable clothing that they don't mind getting messy. Unless required for medical reasons, children should not wear anything on their feet, although slippers should be permitted.

A bottle of water is also advised, especially for use after relaxation activities.

Chapter 3

JELLYFISH CLASSES

Duration

A typical Jellyfish class lasts for one hour. However, this could be made longer or shorter depending on the number of **exploring the theme** activities that are chosen.

How a class works

Jellyfish classes are grouped into blocks. Each block consists of five one-hour class plans; one for each **Jellyfish strand**. Ideally, classes should be delivered in the order in which they appear in the blocks. However, strands from other blocks may also be grouped together to form a series of classes based around the same **Jellyfish strand**. For example, it is possible to deliver all six classes from the **Discover** strand over a course of six sessions. The order in which you teach Jellyfish classes may depend on the requirements of the children you are working with.

The components of each class plan are:

- **Initial gathering**
- **Exploring the theme** (four possible activities)
- **Creative expression**
- **Final gathering**

Class plans can be followed in their entirety and in the order suggested or you may prefer to choose an activity from the plan and deliver it discreetly. However, we would insist that each class begins and ends with the **initial gathering** and **final gathering**, as they mark the beginning and the end of classes.

To support the delivery of Jellyfish classes, all plans, resources and pages marked with a may be photocopied.

Beginning a class

As discussed in the previous chapter, the room should be set up before the child or children enter and music should be playing in the background.

All Jellyfish classes should start in the same way and children should be greeted at the entrance.

Children should be expected to join the class in a quiet, calm manner but may be permitted to whisper. Model the voice volume expected as you greet them and set expectations beforehand.

Direct children to the **gathering place**. In this space children should be asked to form a seated circle around the **focus point**. Allow time to take in the **focus point**, encouraging them to be mindful of where they are and what they are going to be doing.

Ideally, when working with a large group, two adults should be present so that one can greet the children at the door and the other can direct them to the **gathering place**.

The class should not begin until all children are sitting in a circle around the **focus point**. For the first class, the **Jellyfish rules** (see below) should be shared and children should be introduced to the different areas. Use this as an opportunity to model expectations for moving around the space, particularly in the **sensory and relaxation zone**, where they will be trusted to explore and work independently while others are engaged in different activities.

RULES OF BE THE JELLYFISH

★ Respect what you see, hear and experience

★ Contribute to an atmosphere of calm and creativity

★ Participate to the best of your ability

To provide continuity and a feeling of safety and familiarity, the beginning of all classes starts with the **initial gathering**.

Initial gathering (5–10 minutes)

The **initial gathering** takes place in a circle around the **focus point**.

Brushing off

Model how to do this by starting from your head (moving down to your feet) and using the palm of your hands to dust off any unwanted thoughts, feelings or parts of the day. Allow the children to be vocal in expressing some of the things that they are brushing away. Indicate the end of the **brushing off** by finishing and reminding the children that they can now begin the class refreshed.

Now enter into the **Jellyfish breathing exercise**.

Jellyfish breathing exercise

This is an important part of the **initial gathering**, as it helps to calm and quieten even the most excited groups.

Stand tall, arms by sides, feet shoulder width apart and align posture as though a string has been pulled through the crown of the head.

- Model breathing in through the nose and out through the mouth for a count of three. Repeat until all children have joined in. As the rhythm of the group's breathing becomes more consistent, stop counting but continue leading the breathing. Aim for a minimum of five deep breaths.
- Raise both arms slowly and hold at shoulder level. Begin to wave arms alternately up and down; the motion should imitate moving jellyfish tentacles. Aim for at least five repetitions.
- Lean forwards, lowering the head and bending the knees, arms crossed on the chest. Inhale deeply and in one fluid, circular motion, release the arms, sweeping to the side and up above the head where the palms of the hands will meet. Ask children to reach for the sky here and tilt the head upwards. Exhale and allow the arms and head to drop with control and return to starting position. Repeat at least five times.

- Standing tall, bend arms at the elbow and raise to shoulder height. Hands should meet the palms of the person either side without touching. As a group, take a deep breath and one step forward and sweep arms to meet in the centre of the circle. Breathe out taking a step back to the original position. Repeat at least five times.
- Wiggle the body down to 'the bottom of the sea' and into a seated position.

Remember to explain how breathing can be used as a tool to help them feel calm and energized at any time of the day.

Now, in seated position begin the **Jellyfish wave**.

The Jellyfish wave

To create the **Jellyfish wave** ask everyone to hold hands with the person either side of them. Starting with one pair of clasped hands, pass the wave by raising and lowering the arms around the circle. Continue this pattern until the wave has passed through everyone. Each wave sends a good intention for the class, decided by the group or offered by an individual. Children may also like to send around keywords linked to the class theme. Model slow gentle working of the wave to ensure no pulling or jerking of arms occur.

After the last intention (aim for a maximum of five) begin **exploring the theme**.

Exploring the theme (15–20 minutes)

There are four activities to choose from. It is possible to spend all the time on one activity; however, a selection makes for a more varied experience that caters for different learning styles. This section of the class is important to enable as many children as possible to access the theme creatively and with a multi-sensory approach.

The four activities are:

- **Task.** This is an activity specific to the theme and will relate to one of the five **Jellyfish strands** that underpin the social and emotional aim of the class. **Tasks** include role play, games, discussion and mindfulness activities. These may be individual, group or paired. Many **tasks** will require resources, some of which have been provided.

- **Bodywork.** This comprises a number of poses, stretches and movements. These are modelled first by the Jellyfish teacher before the whole class participates. Slow movement, deep breaths and stillness in pose should be encouraged. **Bodywork** has been designed to stretch the body and open the mind to the class theme. Some children may find replication challenging, so praise for participation, focus and effort is essential. An illustration of each bodywork pose listed can be found in the 'Bodywork' section on page 191.

- **Massage.** Linked to the class theme, each routine has at least five strokes. These are not massage stokes in the traditional use of the word; some are modelled, others are open to the individual's interpretation and some are a tactile response to a keyword or story.

  When introducing massage, it is important to be aware this may be the first time that the children have experienced peer massage and firm rules need to be set.

- **Visualization.** Visualization is used as a mindfulness technique but also helps to promote imagination and storytelling. All visualizations are read by the Jellyfish teacher. For this activity children are invited to find a safe space anywhere in the room and lie in a comfortable position. Children may also be seated for a visualization. An explanation of each visualization listed can be found in the 'Visualization' section on page 227.

When the **exploring the theme** section of the class comes to an end, return to the **gathering place** to ready the children for their **creative expression.** This is a good opportunity to recap on the nature of the theme and the possibilities for creativity.

Creative expression (30 minutes)

The aim of **creative expression** is to enable self-expression in response to the theme of the class. This should be of the child's own instigation so that it is their own personal communication. However, for many children, regardless of age, this freedom of expression can be overwhelming and limit the effectiveness of the class. For this reason, Be the Jellyfish offers a differentiated approach to **creative expression** to help meet the needs of all children. It is essential to place emphasis on the importance of there being no right or wrong when it comes to **creative expression**. This is the **Jellyfish motto**.

Children may be guided in their choice of materials and be allowed to discuss possibilities for what they would like to achieve. However, it is imperative that Jellyfish teachers do not lead or tell children specifically what to create. Individuals should be free to choose their own colours, patterns, marks and materials. Ensure personal vision is not encroached upon and preconceived ideas are not imposed.

Some children may not wish to use the art materials and should then be directed toward the **sensory and relaxation zone**. It is important to remember that **creative expression** can also be met using some of the resources available in this area, such as the sand or dough.

While the children are working, the opportunity for **creative chatter** may arise.

Creative chatter

The conversation between Jellyfish teachers and children, or indeed child-to-child, is known as **creative chatter**. **Creative chatter** is the process of talking to a participant about what has been created in a polite, accepting, non-judgemental manner and without interpretation. **Creative chatter** is entirely optional and no child is obliged to talk about their creation or the activity they have engaged themselves in. It is simply an invitation to share and discuss aspects of their work if they so wish. Simply being present when a child is creating, or creating alongside them, can be equally powerful.

Start by inviting the child to talk about their work. **Creative chatter** may be instigated using sentence openers such as: 'Tell me about what you have created…', 'I'm interested in…', 'I notice that…' Jellyfish teachers should also feel confident to use their own intuition and curiosity when chatting.

Alternatively, use the guidance questions that accompany each class plan. These are often geared towards the template provided in the **creative expression** options; however, they may also be used and adapted for any of the other **creative expression** activities. Questions are divided into two categories: **on the shore** and **under the sea**. **On the shore** questions are intended to open conversation; **under the sea** questions help to develop discussion further. **Creative chatter** can help children to talk about any difficult thoughts and feelings that they might have about themselves, others or situations. However, it is essential to recognize that not all **creative expression** is a metaphor and should not be interpreted as such.

Something to remember

You are primarily a respectful listener and a polite observer. The role of a Jellyfish teacher is not to counsel, give advice, criticize or make judgements. Instead, they should listen only to what the child is telling them and must not lead or ask probing questions. Common relaxation and mindfulness tools and techniques may however be offered if deemed appropriate.

If necessary, determine whether a child requires more than what Jellyfish classes are intended for. If a disclosure is made by a child, or it is felt that a child is in any danger, it is the responsibility of the Jellyfish teacher to follow the Child Protection protocol.

Final gathering

It is likely that children will complete their **creative expression** at different times. Children should be informed of how much time they will have and be notified as to when that time is almost over. A ten-minute warning prior to the end of **creative expression** is useful and should be followed by a one-minute countdown to ensure everybody is back in the **gathering place** to conclude the class.

As children complete their **creative expression**, they should be invited to bring their work to the **gathering place**. Once the children have gathered with their work, there are a number of ways to share and appreciate what has been presented. These options include:

- **A moving gallery.** Children form a ring around the **focus point** and their **creative expression** and move clockwise together followed by moving anti-clockwise. By forming a ring around the work they are collectively appreciating and accepting everyone's personal interpretation of the theme. Children may make positive comments and observations about the **creative expression** they are viewing.
- **Peer appreciation.** Children remain seated on their cushion and are invited to make a positive comment on another's work.
- **Observation shower.** Children form a stationary ring around the **focus point** and **creative expression**. They are then invited to use superlatives to shower the work with appreciation. More than one person may speak at the same time.
- **Silent reflection.** Children remain seated on their cushions and take a moment to reflect on the variations of **creative expression** presented. This time should be used to emphasize the **Jellyfish motto** of there being 'no right or wrong'.

- **Personal offerings.** Children remain seated on their cushions and are invited to share their **creative expression** with the group. If many children wish to share, they could show their work to a partner or present it within a small group.

To finish the class, the **Jellyfish gift cards** should be passed around the group. Once a child has taken a card they are permitted to leave the circle and for that individual the class has finished. Children do not have to take a card if they do not wish to.

Each **Jellyfish gift card** displays a positive word for the children to take away with them. This word is chosen at random and should be considered as a quality to think about, work on, acquire or, if it is one that the child feels they already possess, to give thanks for.

The **Jellyfish gift cards** are available to download from www.jkp.com/voucher using the code CREEJELLYFISH

Everyday positivity tools and techniques

To promote positive wellbeing within and outside of Jellyfish classes, below are several well-known suggestions Jellyfish teachers may wish to pass on to children.

These are common relaxation and mindfulness techniques used to support children's general wellbeing and are not given as professional medical or therapeutic advice.

- Deep breaths
- Count to ten/back from ten
- Positive self-talk/affirmations
- Self-massage
- Write thoughts down
- Draw a picture/doodle/colour
- Talk to someone you trust
- Take a walk/exercise
- Do something kind for yourself or another
- Smile
- Visualize

- Sing/hum
- Tense and release muscles
- Focus on a point
- Repeat a word or mantra in your mind
- Manipulate dough or use a fidget object

Block 1

CLASS PLANS AND RESOURCES

BLOCK 1:1

Theme: JELLYFISH

Strand: DISCOVER

The Jellyfish themed class forms the core of Be the Jellyfish. It is the first theme that children are introduced to and can be revisited as often as you wish. A useful activity is to repeat this theme over a series of weeks or at the beginning of each new term so that a collection of jellyfish themed material is created. A personal journey can then be discovered and mapped. This theme is the vehicle for the Discover Jellyfish strand and so enables us to discover safely how we see ourselves, relationships with others and the world around us.

Initial gathering: brushing off/Jellyfish breathing/Jellyfish wave

Exploring the theme: choose from...

Task	Bodywork
Each child is given a **Jellyfish picture card**. They introduce the jellyfish on their card to a partner and say how the jellyfish is feeling today. The partner is then invited to ask the jellyfish some questions. These could be basic questions, e.g. What is your name? Where do you live? Or they could be more complex questions, e.g. What has made you feel ____________ today? Repeat activity with the partner introducing their **Jellyfish picture card**. This activity should be modelled by the Jellyfish teacher before handing out the cards.	★ Jellyfish bell ★ Bobbing jellyfish ★ Darting jellyfish ★ Wibbly wobbly jellyfish ★ Resting jellyfish
Massage	**Visualization**
★ **Permission, hug and frame** ★ Waves of the sea ★ Shape of jellyfish ★ Pattern on jellyfish ★ Tentacles ★ Draw how the jellyfish is feeling today ★ **Personal signature and hug**	**See Jellyfish visualization**

Creative expression: to support children to discover aspects of themselves, you may like to:

- ★ Provide the **jellyfish template**
- ★ Invite children to use half a paper plate to create their own jellyfish
- ★ Allow free choice

Final gathering: Jellyfish gallery

Questions to support creative chatter:

On the shore

- ★ If this jellyfish had a name, what would it be?
- ★ Where does this jellyfish live?
- ★ What makes this jellyfish happy? (Change emotion to excited, loved, sad, frightened…)

Under the sea

- ★ How is this jellyfish feeling right now?
- ★ If you could change something about this jellyfish, what would it be?
- ★ What is special about this jellyfish?

BLOCK 1:2

Theme: **ELEMENTS** Strand: **EXPLORE**

The Elements theme is the vehicle to the Explore Jellyfish strand. Through Explore we seek to find out more about what we have discovered and hope to gain a greater understanding and appreciation of who we are. The elements of earth, wind, fire and water have different qualities and characteristics that can be related to and explored.

Initial gathering: brushing off/Jellyfish breathing/Jellyfish wave

Exploring the theme: choose from...

Task	**Bodywork**
Using a play parachute (or large sheet of fabric) ask the children to form a circle and take hold of the parachute with two hands. Explore how elements behave by working as a group to create movements such as calm/powerful waves, dancing flames, firm/crumbling earth, gentle breeze/fierce winds. Let your imagination run wild; there are so many games and activities that you can do using the parachute with the Elements theme. Consider what is best for your group.	★ Fire one ★ Fire two ★ Wind ★ Earth ★ Water
Massage	**Visualization**
★ **Permission, hug and frame** ★ Our planet ★ Flickering flame ★ Gusts of wind ★ Cracked earth ★ Moving waves ★ **Personal signature and hug**	**See Elements visualization**

Creative expression: to support children to explore different emotions, you may like to:

- ★ Provide the **box template**
- ★ Invite children to choose an element, or elements, that they are drawn to and create an image using different mediums to represent this
- ★ Allow free choice

Final gathering: Jellyfish gallery

Questions to support creative chatter:

On the shore

- ★ Which element/elements are here?
- ★ How could these elements be described?
- ★ Which feeling/s could be associated with this element/these elements?

Under the sea

- ★ Which element are you most drawn to and why?
- ★ Which words come to mind when you see this element/these elements?
- ★ What could this element/these elements do?

BLOCK 1:3

Theme: **MUSIC**

Strand: **EXPRESS**

The Music theme is the vehicle to the Express Jellyfish strand. Express invites us to explore the possibilities of our imagination, our thoughts and our feelings. Music can have a profound effect on our feelings and emotions; it can conjure images, help recall memories and enable creative expression.

Initial gathering: brushing off/Jellyfish breathing/Jellyfish wave

Exploring the theme: choose from...

Task	Bodywork
Prepare large sheets of paper and a selection of different music (including at least one classical piece). Tell the children that you are going to play them some music and invite them to respond to it on the paper using art materials. Children are to use one medium at a time but may change it at regular intervals, e.g. a green chalk, a red felt tip pen. Ask them to look for shapes and patterns on the paper and comment on the art they have created. Try to help them verbalize what it was about the music that urged them to make the marks they did.	★ Ear ★ Sound wave ★ Treble clef ★ Crochet ★ Line of music
Massage	**Visualization**
★ **Permission, hug and frame** ★ Sound waves ★ Drums ★ Guitar strings ★ Piano keys ★ DJ ★ **Personal signature and hug**	**See Music visualization**

Creative expression: to support children to express themselves through musical response, you may like to:

- ★ Provide the **music bar template** or **music line template** for children to make their own music. The children could add musical notes or even images of objects, events or people they associate with music to these
- ★ Invite children to use images of music or instruments to make a collage
- ★ Allow free choice

Final gathering: Jellyfish gallery

Questions to support creative chatter:

On the shore

- ★ How might this music sound?
- ★ When might this music be played?
- ★ How might this music make a listener feel?

Under the sea

- ★ In what situation would you expect to hear this music?
- ★ What would other people say about this music?
- ★ If this music were to remind you of anything, what might that be?

BLOCK 1:4

Theme: **TREASURE**

Strand: **MANAGE**

The Treasure theme is the vehicle to the Manage Jellyfish strand. Manage helps us to acknowledge thoughts, feelings and situations safely. The things, people and memories we treasure, be they physical, mental or spiritual, are so specific and personal to each and every one of us, that to acknowledge them can provide us with great strength and reassurance.

Initial gathering: brushing off/Jellyfish breathing/Jellyfish wave

Exploring the theme: choose from...

Task	Bodywork
Show the children an empty treasure box. Explain that the box will be able to hold all the things that are precious to them. Brainstorm possibilities. Next, open the box and mime placing your own treasure into it. Invite children to do the same as the box is passed around the circle. Children may share what they have put in it (as you may do) or keep it a secret. Once everyone has placed an imaginary treasure in the box, close the lid and place the box on the **focus point**.	★ Receive ★ Cherish ★ Contain ★ Hide ★ Reveal
Massage	**Visualization**
★ **Permission, hug and frame** ★ Treasure chest ★ Gold coins ★ Gemstones ★ Pearls ★ Lock the treasure chest ★ **Personal signature and hug**	**See Treasure visualization**

Creative expression: to support children to manage the things that are precious to them, you may like to:

- ★ Provide the **treasure chest template**
- ★ Invite children to decorate a special treasure box
- ★ Allow free choice

Final gathering: Jellyfish gallery

Questions to support creative chatter:

On the shore

- ★ What is this treasure?
- ★ Who does this treasure belong to?
- ★ Where is this treasure hidden?

Under the sea

- ★ Why is this treasure precious?
- ★ How is this treasure protected?
- ★ How does it feel to know that this treasure is safe?

BLOCK 1:5

Theme: FANTASY

Strand: DEVELOP

The Fantasy theme is the vehicle to the Develop Jellyfish strand. Develop helps us to grow as individuals, in our relationships and in our lives. It helps us to explore possibilities, move forwards and make changes for the better. The world of fantasy is an ideal platform for growth; the possibilities of fantasy are endless, as is our ability to develop who we are through the choices we make.

Initial gathering: brushing off/Jellyfish breathing/Jellyfish wave

Exploring the theme: choose from...

Task	**Bodywork**
Give each child a card from the **fantasy beginning and ending cards**. Children move around the space in order to find someone who has a beginning or ending that could match their card. Once they have found a partner, they return to the **gathering place** and pairs may then share their card match with the group. Remember there is no right or wrong answer to matches, although some matches may be more obvious.	★ Giant ★ Witch's hat ★ Fairy ★ Unicorn ★ Pegasus
Massage	**Visualization**
★ **Permission, hug and frame** ★ Castle ★ Sword ★ Shield ★ Unicorn ★ Crown ★ **Personal signature and hug**	**See Fantasy visualization**

Creative expression: to support children to develop an alternative world, you may like to:

- ★ Provide a protective **shield template**
- ★ Invite children to create a mini story book
- ★ Allow free choice

Final gathering: Jellyfish gallery

Questions to support creative chatter:

On the shore

- ★ Whose shield is this?
- ★ What is this shield made from?
- ★ In what situation could a shield like this be used?

Under the sea

- ★ How would it feel to be able to use this shield?
- ★ What would you do if you had a shield like this?
- ★ If you could choose another item or a fantasy character to go with this shield, what would you choose?

BLOCK 1: RESOURCES

Theme	Task	Bodywork	Massage	Visualization	Creative expression
Jellyfish	Jellyfish picture cards	Jellyfish	As listed on class plans	Jellyfish	Jellyfish template Paper plates
Elements	Play parachute	Elements		Elements	Box template
Music	Paper sheets Prepared music	Music		Music	Music bar template Music line template Images of music or instruments Prepared music
Treasure	Treasure box	Treasure		Treasure	Treasure chest template Boxes to decorate
Fantasy	Beginning and ending cards	Fantasy		Fantasy	Shield template

Highlighted items are provided in this book: resources are at the end of this block, massage suggestions are included in the class plans, and bodywork illustrations and visualization outlines are listed at the end of the book.

JELLYFISH B1:1 JELLYFISH TEMPLATE

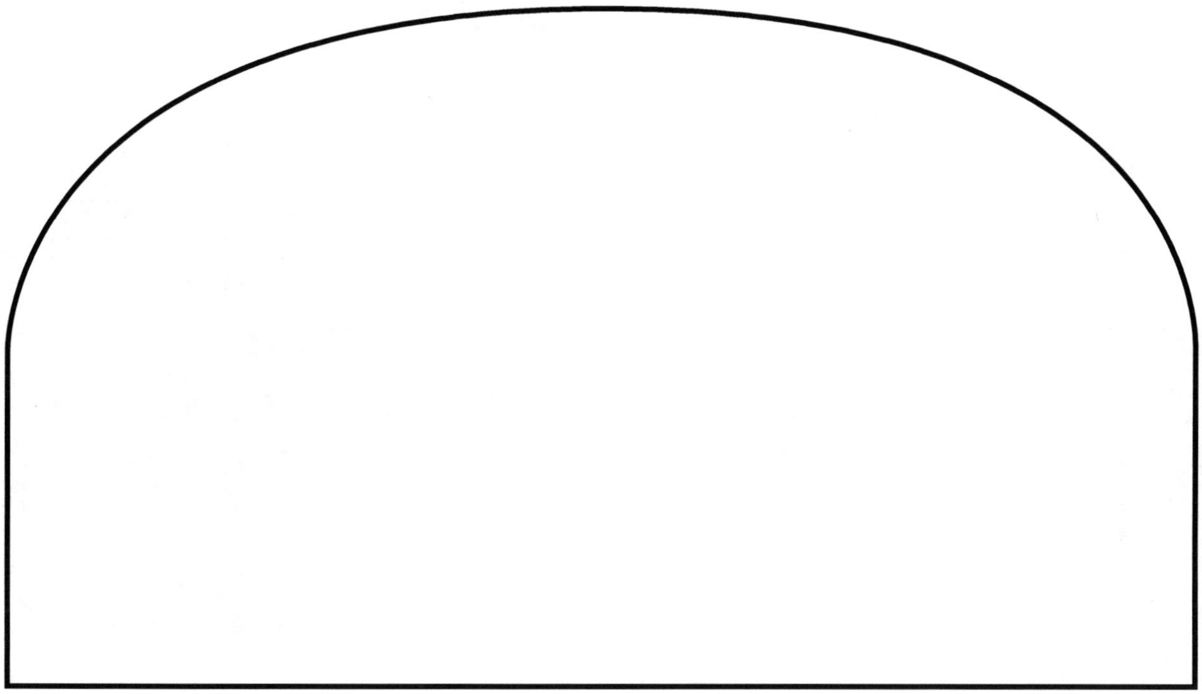

ELEMENTS B1:2 BOX TEMPLATE

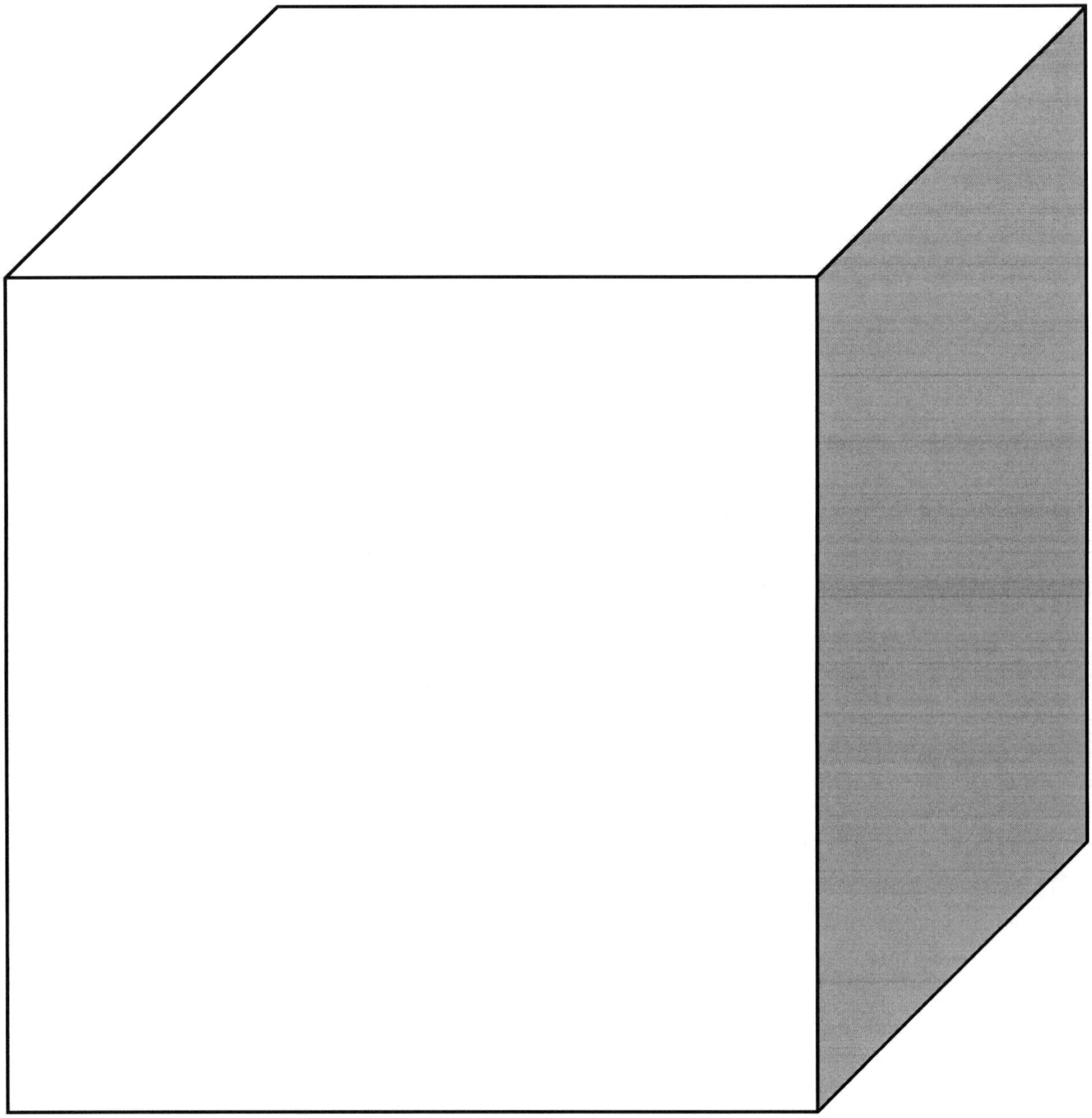

MUSIC B1:3 MUSIC BAR TEMPLATE

MUSIC B1:3 MUSIC LINE TEMPLATE

TREASURE B1:4 TREASURE CHEST TEMPLATE

FANTASY B1:5 BEGINNING AND ENDING CARDS

A spoilt princess...	who ate baked beans for the rest of their life.
A fearsome dragon...	who became loved by all.
A magical unicorn...	who changed their name to Fluffy Pop Pop.

A ragged young girl...	who married an astronaut.
A wicked witch...	who discovered what friendship really meant.
A lonely frog...	who won the lottery.

A friendly ghost...	who lived happily ever after.
A brave knight...	who lived out their days in comfort.
A terrifying monster...	who went to live on the moon.

An evil wizard...	who was never seen again.
A homeless beggar...	who opened a successful coffee shop.
A wandering musician...	who found fame and fortune at the theatre.

A warrior queen...

who continued to believe in fairies.

A talented shoemaker...

who ruled over many far and distant galaxies.

A clever cat...

who became the Prime Minister of Britain.

FANTASY B1:5 SHIELD TEMPLATE

JELLYFISH B1:1 JELLYFISH PICTURE CARDS

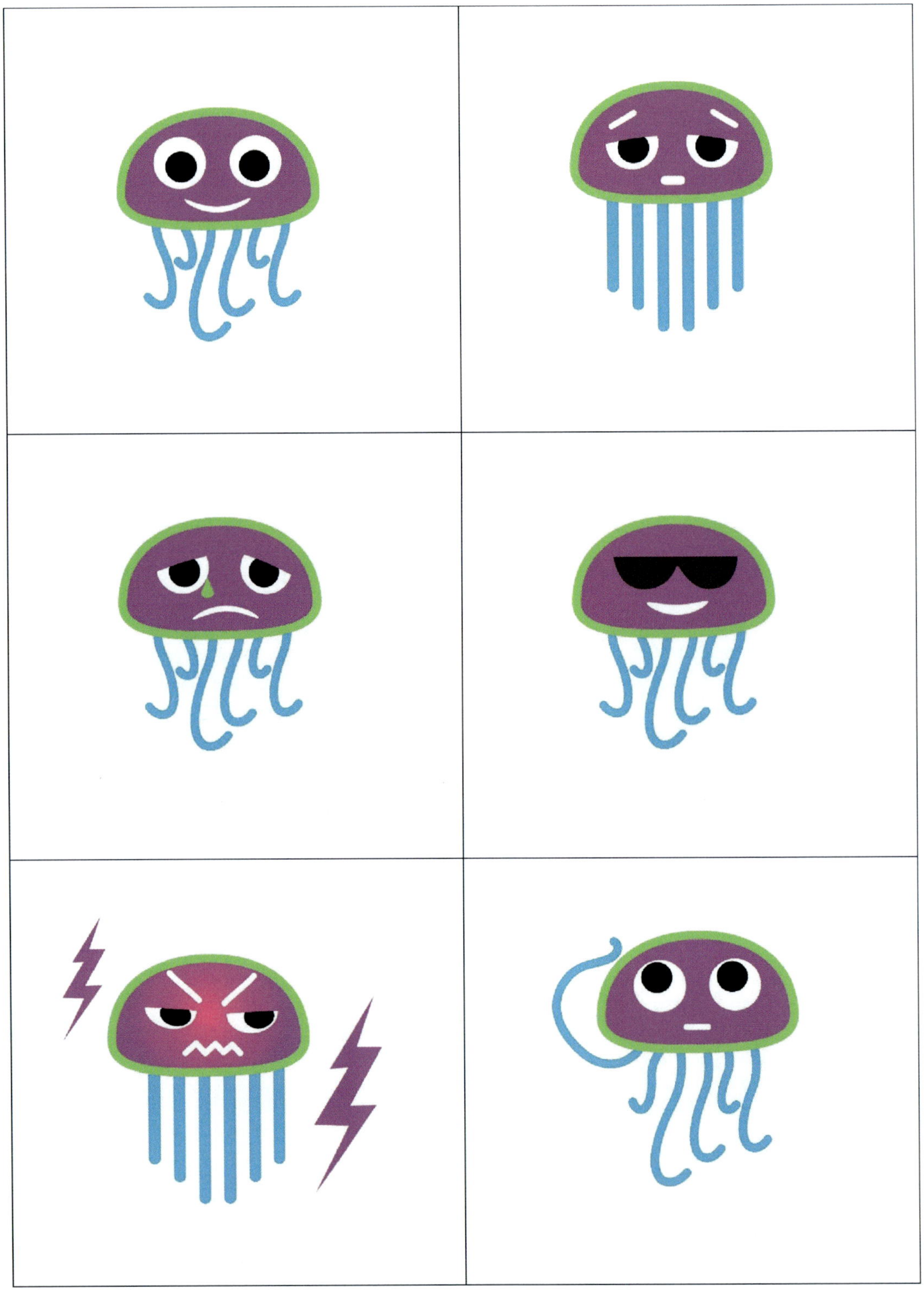

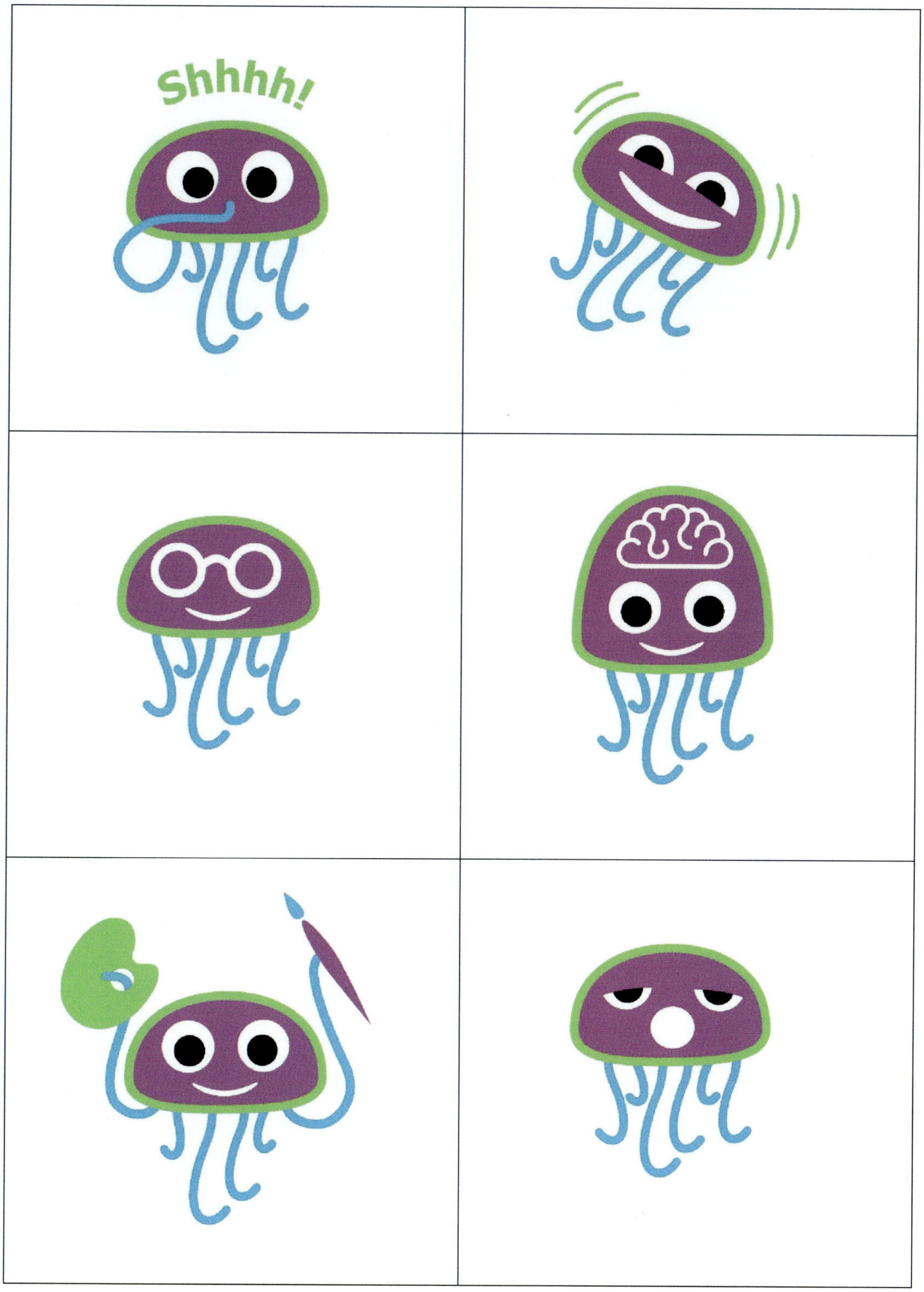
Shhhh!

COLOUR B2:1 HAPPY EMOTION FACES

COLOUR B2:1 SAD EMOTION FACES

COLOUR B2:1 UNSURE EMOTION FACES

COLOUR B2:1 PLEASED EMOTION FACES

COLOUR B2:1 ANGRY EMOTION FACES

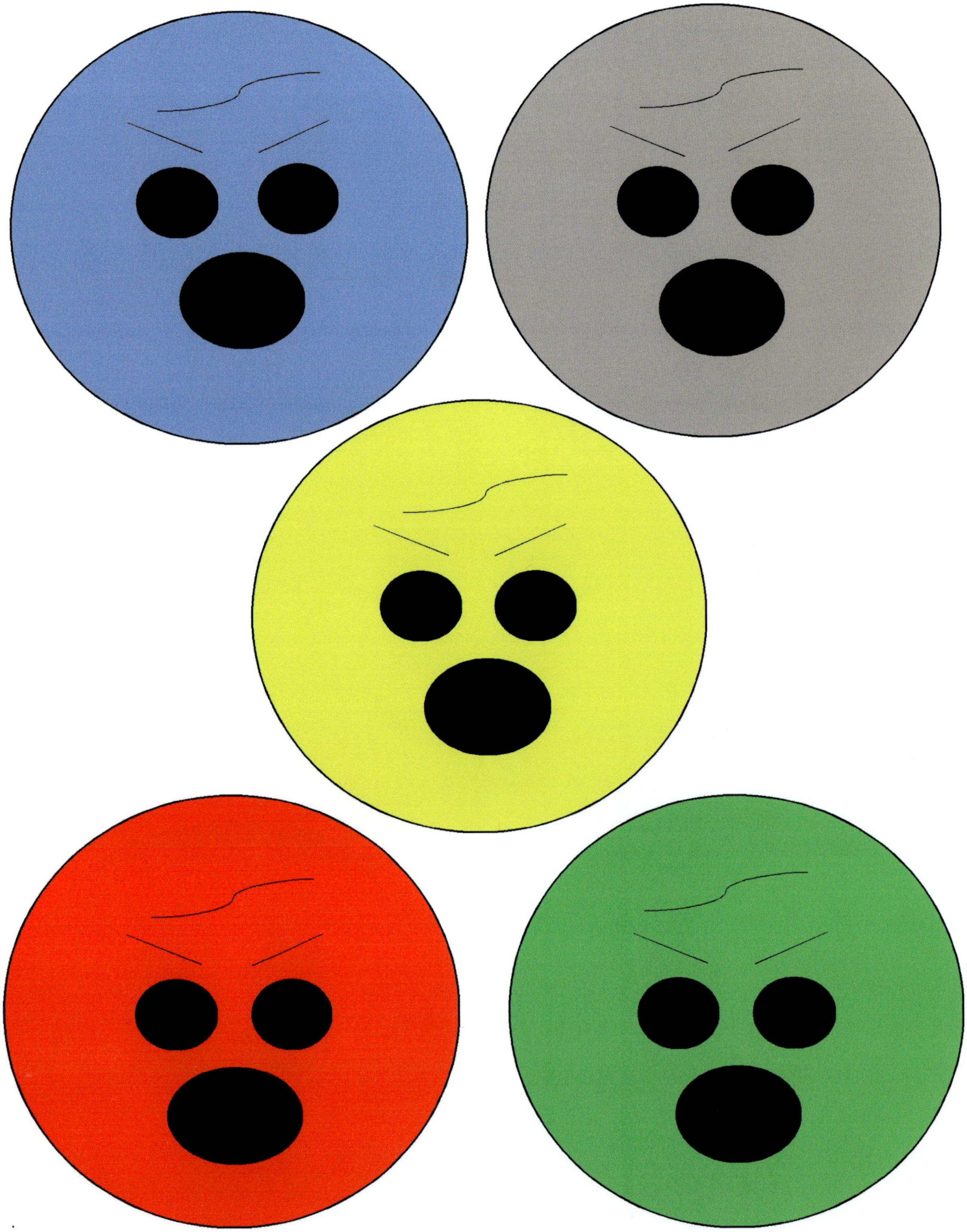

Block 2

CLASS PLANS AND RESOURCES

BLOCK 2:1

Theme: **COLOUR**

Strand: **DISCOVER**

The Colour theme is the vehicle to the Discover Jellyfish strand. Discover is an opportunity to find out about ourselves, relationships with others and the world around us. Colour can be closely associated with emotions and so through this theme, feelings and emotions can be identified and named in a secure setting.

Initial gathering: brushing off/Jellyfish breathing/Jellyfish wave

Exploring the theme: choose from...

Task	Bodywork
Discuss with the children the power of colour. Which colour do they think of when asked about specific occasions, for example: Christmas, Halloween, Easter, birthdays, etc.? Using the **emotion faces**, begin with the happy emotion and invite five children to each hold a face. The group then decides which face looks strongest/weakest of that emotion (this could be done by vote); encourage the children to explain their choices in relation to the colour. Repeat using the other **emotion faces**.	★ Squat down (to collect a colour from the ground) ★ Scoop up a colour ★ Colour to heart ★ Colour to head ★ Rain colour down **Repeat for different colours**
Massage	**Visualization**
★ **Permission, hug and frame** ★ Red dots ★ Blue zigzags ★ Yellow swirls ★ Green lines ★ Purple stars ★ **Personal signature and hug**	**See Colours visualization**

Creative expression: to support children to discover colour as a medium to represent and alter emotions, you may like to:

- ★ Provide the **palette template** (any colours may be used)
- ★ Invite children to create a mood board using different mediums, shades, techniques or a colour
- ★ Allow free choice

Final gathering: Jellyfish gallery

Questions to support creative chatter:

On the shore

- ★ Which is your favourite colour and why?
- ★ Why have these colours been chosen?
- ★ When could this colour/colours be used?

Under the sea

- ★ Which feeling could each colour represent?
- ★ What sort of picture could be painted using this palette?
- ★ If you could take one colour with you, which would it be and why?

BLOCK 2:2

Theme: SPECIAL PLACES

Strand: EXPLORE

The Special Places theme is the vehicle to the Explore Jellyfish strand. Through Explore we seek to gain a greater understanding of who we are and what is important to us. Exploring a special place can help us to identify aspects of what we need in our lives and what we desire to be happy.

Initial gathering: brushing off/Jellyfish breathing/Jellyfish wave

Exploring the theme: choose from...

Task	**Bodywork**
Invite the children to use the **scroll template** to write or draw the things that they would like to have in their special place. Older children may wish to use the **special writing characters** to keep their ideas private. Once completed, invite the children to roll up their scroll and tie it with ribbon. Scrolls are then placed in the **focus point** where a special basket has been prepared; this is the group special place for the duration of the lesson.	★ Safe ★ Rested ★ Secure ★ Peaceful ★ Be yourself
Massage	**Visualization**
★ **Permission, hug and frame** ★ Key to special place ★ Unlock special place ★ Walk into special place ★ Feelings in special place ★ Lock special place ★ **Personal signature and hug**	**See Special Places visualization**

Creative expression: to support children to explore a safe, secure place, you may like to:

- ★ Provide the **door template** that leads to a special place
- ★ Invite children to depict an existing/imaginary special place
- ★ Allow free choice

Final gathering: Jellyfish gallery

Questions to support creative chatter:

On the shore

- ★ Which special place does this door lead to?
- ★ Is the place imaginary or somewhere real?
- ★ Why is this special place special?

Under the sea

- ★ What do you like best about this special place?
- ★ Who might this special place belong to?
- ★ If you could take something from this special place what would it be?

BLOCK 2:3

Theme: DREAMS

Strand: EXPRESS

The Dreams theme is the vehicle to the Express Jellyfish strand. Express invites us to explore the possibilities of our imagination, our thoughts and our feelings. By expressing our dreams, we are free to communicate what it is we want for ourselves, our families, our friends and the world as a whole.

Initial gathering: brushing off/Jellyfish breathing/Jellyfish wave

Exploring the theme: choose from…

Task	Bodywork
Use masking tape, or something similar, to create a dream catcher on the floor (think giant spider's web). Provide the children with the **small cloud templates** and explain that they are to write or draw anything that makes them feel sad, frightened, worried or angry. These can be real or imaginary. Invite the children to place their clouds in the dream catcher so that they have been identified and acknowledged, yet safely caught. Now that the children recognize that there is a way to catch all the unpleasant dreams, encourage them to think of the dreams that they would like to have. Our dreams can now be what we make them, so let's dream! Allow time for children to think and share their dreams with the group.	★ Fly ★ Climb ★ Invisible ★ Royal ★ Mermaid
Massage	**Visualization**
★ **Permission, hug and frame** ★ Sleepy zzzzzzzz ★ Fluffy clouds ★ Twinkling lights ★ Dream bubbles ★ Catch the dreams ★ **Personal signature and hug**	**See Dreams visualization**

Creative expression: to support children to express their inner self, hopes and fears, you may like to:

- ★ Provide the **cloud template**
- ★ Invite them to create their own dream catcher
- ★ Allow free choice

Final gathering: Jellyfish gallery

Questions to support creative chatter:

On the shore

- ★ Is this a good dream or a bad dream?
- ★ Is this a day dream or a night dream?
- ★ Whose dream could this be?

Under the sea

- ★ What is happening in this dream?
- ★ What do you think or feel about this dream?
- ★ If this dream could be changed, how would you choose to change it?

BLOCK 2:4

Theme: MAGIC

Strand: MANAGE

The Magic theme is the vehicle to the Manage Jellyfish strand. Manage helps us to acknowledge thoughts, feelings and situations safely. The idea of magic can be powerful, as it enables us to envisage and safely contain unwanted thoughts, feelings and situations without denying their existence. It also enables us to acquire things we may feel we need in order to move forwards.

Initial gathering: brushing off/Jellyfish breathing/Jellyfish wave

Exploring the theme: choose from...

Task	**Bodywork**
Provide each child with a small bottle or jar with a lid. Give them a piece of paper on which to write something that they wish to improve on. This should be something personal to them. Once written, children roll and place the scrolls into a container and add some 'magical' ingredients such as feathers, sequins and glitter to complete the potion. Potions may then be displayed on or around the **focus point** until the end of the class.	★ Magic star ★ Magic broom ★ Magic potion ★ Magic wand ★ Magic book
Massage	**Visualization**
★ **Permission, hug and frame** ★ Wand ★ Spell book ★ Potion ★ Broom stick ★ Cobweb ★ **Personal signature and hug**	**See Magic visualization**

Creative expression: to support children to manage emotions, feelings or traits, you may like to:

- ★ Provide the **cauldron template**
- ★ Invite children to make a magical object
- ★ Allow free choice

Final gathering: Jellyfish gallery

Questions to support creative chatter:

On the shore

- ★ Who could this cauldron belong to?
- ★ What is in this cauldron?
- ★ What could this cauldron be used for?

Under the sea

- ★ Are the contents of this cauldron good or bad or somewhere in the middle?
- ★ How would the contents of this cauldron make someone feel?
- ★ If you could add additional ingredients to this cauldron, what would they be?

BLOCK 2:5

Theme: **CHARACTERS**

Strand: **DEVELOP**

The Characters theme is the vehicle to the Develop Jellyfish strand. Develop helps us to grow as individuals, in our relationships and in our lives. It helps us to explore possibilities, move forwards and make changes for the better. Through exploring a variety of characters the diversity of humankind is revealed and accepted. This allows us to accept and develop who we are.

Initial gathering: brushing off/Jellyfish breathing/Jellyfish wave

Exploring the theme: choose from…

Task	**Bodywork**
Invite children to take a character **word card** and ask for a volunteer to act out their character to the group. The group has up to three guesses before the character is revealed. Once the character is known to the group, the character is welcomed and applauded. This can also be done in small groups of children, especially if some children feel uncomfortable about acting in front of the whole group.	★ Confident ★ In love ★ Shy ★ Old ★ Angry
Massage	**Visualization**
★ **Permission, hug and frame** ★ A cook's hat ★ A footballer's ball ★ A teacher's spectacles ★ A baby's bottle ★ A superhero's badge ★ **Personal signature and hug**	**See Characters visualization**

Creative expression: to support children to develop their own character, you may like to:

- ★ Provide a human template
- ★ Invite them to design their own character
- ★ Allow free choice

Final gathering: Jellyfish gallery

Questions to support creative chatter:

On the shore

- ★ Who is this character?
- ★ Where does this character live?
- ★ Can you tell me one thing that is wonderful about this character?

Under the sea

- ★ What quality do you like in this character?
- ★ If this character could speak, what would it say?
- ★ How do you feel about this character?

BLOCK 2: RESOURCES

Theme	Task	Bodywork	Massage	Visualization	Creative expression
Colour	Emotion faces	Colour	As listed on class plans	Colour	Palette template
Special Places	Scroll template Special writing characters Ribbon and basket	Special Places		Special Places	Door template
Dreams	Masking tape Cloud template	Dreams		Dreams	Cloud template
Magic	Bottle or jar Paper Feathers, sequins and/or glitter	Magic		Magic	Cauldron template
Characters	Word cards	Characters		Characters	Human template

Highlighted items are provided in this book: resources are at the end of this block, massage suggestions are included in the class plans, and bodywork illustrations and visualization outlines are listed at the end of the book.

COLOUR B2:1 PALETTE TEMPLATE

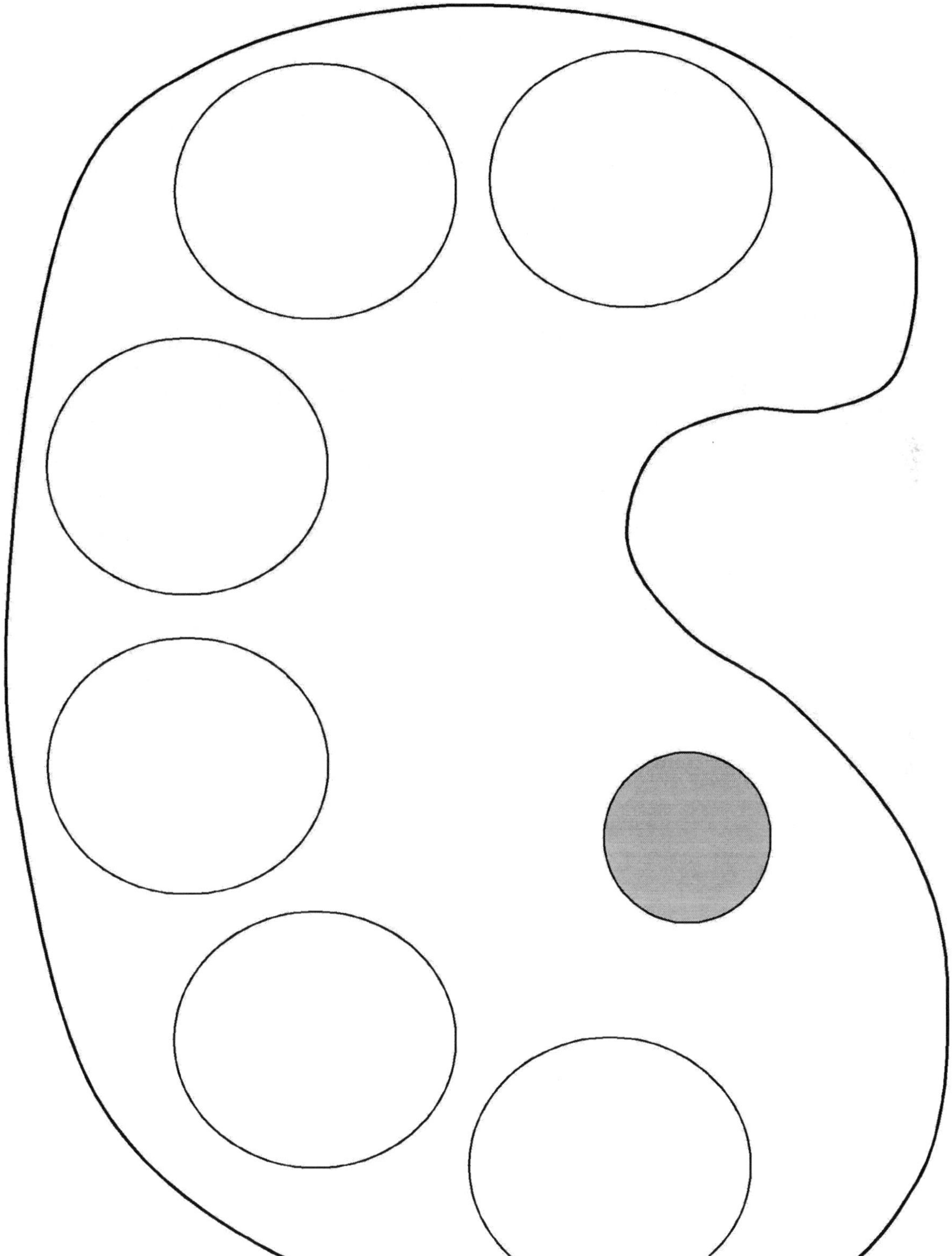

SPECIAL PLACES B2:2 SCROLL TEMPLATE

SPECIAL PLACES B2:2 SPECIAL WRITING CHARACTERS

a	ꝸ
b	θ
c	≡
d	◊
e	Ͽ
f	⤷
g	∧
h	◎
i	+
j	∨
k	Σ
l	☆
m	$

n	△
o	ɷ
p	⋮
q	☾
r	≈
s	∞
t	ǂ
u	∩
v	♈
w	╲
x	♡
y	⊙
z	⊥

SPECIAL PLACES B2:2 DOOR TEMPLATE

DREAMS B2:3 SMALL CLOUD TEMPLATES

DREAMS B2:3 CLOUD TEMPLATE

MAGIC B2:4 CAULDRON TEMPLATE

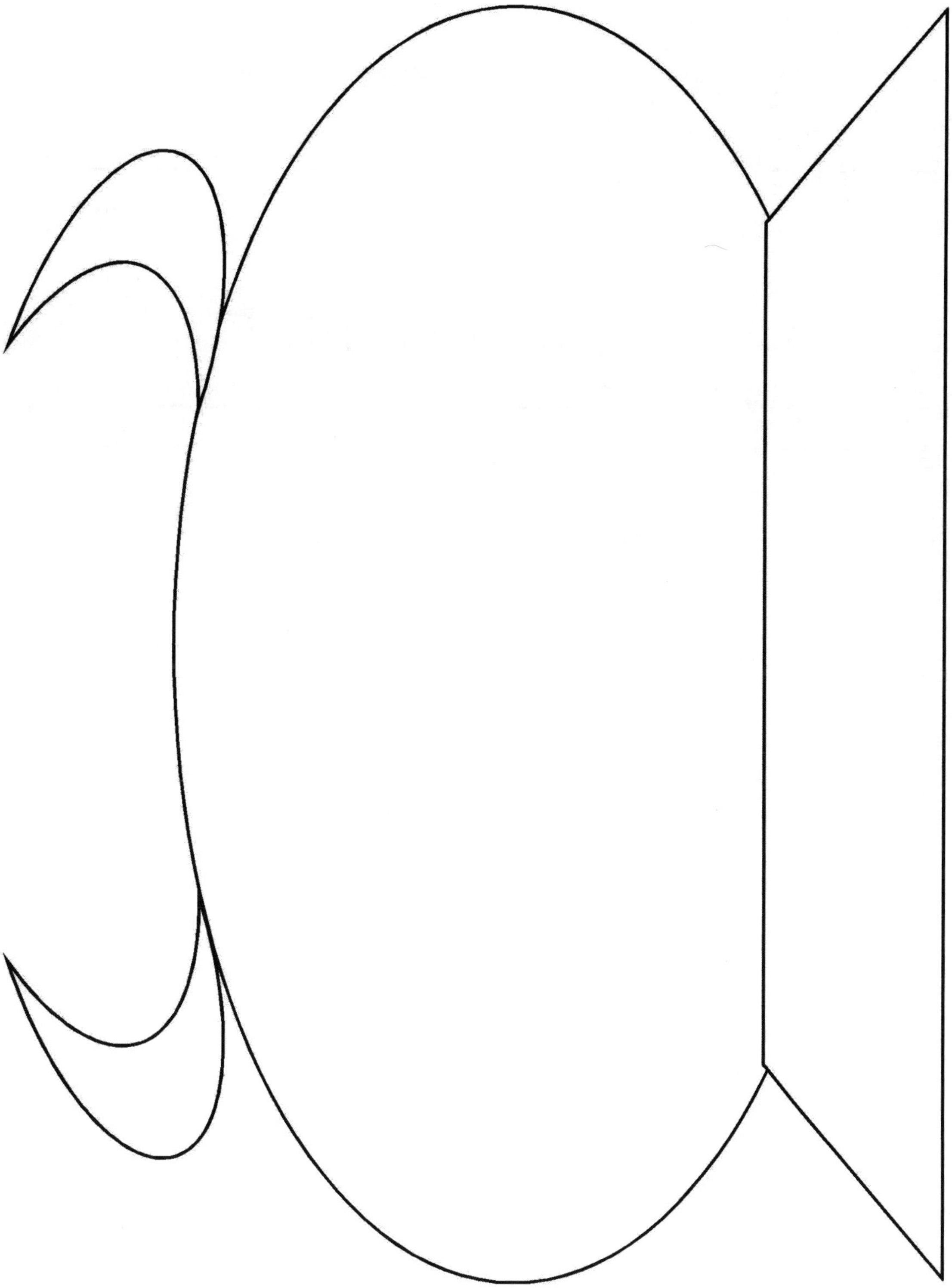

CHARACTERS B2:5 WORD CARDS

A grandparent
A teacher
A clown
A singer
A shy child
A king

A ballerina

A bully

A superhero

A footballer

A baby

A burglar

A musician
A robot
A life guard
A cook
A doctor
A soldier

Block 3

CLASS PLANS AND RESOURCES

✱

BLOCK 3:1

Theme: **ANIMALS**

Strand: **DISCOVER**

The Animals theme is the vehicle to the Discover Jellyfish strand. Discover is an opportunity to find out about ourselves, our relationship with others and the world around us. Animals come in all shapes and sizes, have varying behaviours, perceived personality traits and qualities; this makes them an ideal theme for discovery.

Initial gathering: brushing off/Jellyfish breathing/Jellyfish wave

Exploring the theme: choose from...

Task	Bodywork
Begin by taking and reading a **What am I? card**. Rather than asking the group to name what they believe the animal to be, invite them individually to form the shape or pose of the animal they think the card is describing. On the count of three, instruct everyone to make the noise of the animal they think has been described. Were they correct? Repeat, inviting children to read the cards if they wish to do so.	★ Tiger ★ Mouse ★ Swan ★ Frog ★ Giraffe
Massage	**Visualization**
★ **Permission, hug and frame** ★ Kangaroo hops ★ Slithering snake ★ Cat paws ★ Bird wings ★ Elephant walk ★ **Personal signature and hug**	**See Animals visualization**

Creative expression: to support children to discover some of their own characteristics or those that they would like to acquire, you may like to:

- ★ Provide children with a choice of animal figures to draw
- ★ Invite children to make a collage about an animal or multiple animals
- ★ Allow free choice

Final gathering: Jellyfish gallery

Questions to support creative chatter:

On the shore

- ★ Where does this animal live?
- ★ Does this animal have fur, feathers, a shell or something else?
- ★ What does this animal like doing?

Under the sea

- ★ What is this animal most proud of?
- ★ What is this animal least proud of?
- ★ How does this animal feel about themselves?

BLOCK 3:2

Theme: **DEEP SPACE**

Strand: **EXPLORE**

The Deep Space theme is the vehicle to the Explore Jellyfish strand. Through Explore we seek to find out more about what we have discovered and hope to gain a greater understanding and appreciation of who we are. Deep Space allows for true exploration of self and through the metaphor of planets and stars, relationships with others, past, present and future can be explored.

Initial gathering: brushing off/Jellyfish breathing/Jellyfish wave

Exploring the theme: choose from...

Task	Bodywork
Give each child a **planet template** on which to create their own planet. Ask them also to include their name somewhere on the planet. Each planet should then be cut out. Once the children are ready, tell them that they are now going to form part of a Jellyfish solar system with the **focus point** acting as the sun. Ask each child to place their planet somewhere in the room and tell them that their planet can be any distance from the sun and any distance from other planets. Once all the planets have been placed in the Jellyfish solar system invite the children to explain why they have chosen that position for their planet.	★ Sun star ★ Planet ★ Shooting star ★ Big Dipper ★ Orion's Belt
Massage	**Visualization**
★ **Permission, hug and frame** ★ A universe with stars ★ Moon, full/half ★ Planets ★ Shooting stars ★ Circling galaxies ★ **Personal signature and hug**	**See Deep Space visualization**

Creative expression: to support children to explore relationships, you may like to:

- ★ Provide the **solar system template**
- ★ Invite children to make their own 3D planets using clay
- ★ Allow free choice

Final gathering: Jellyfish gallery

Questions to support creative chatter:

On the shore

- ★ Which is the most important planet in this solar system?
- ★ Which is the least important planet in this solar system?
- ★ How does the sun help or hinder this solar system?

Under the sea

- ★ How do the planets feel about their position in this solar system?
- ★ What do the planets think about one another?
- ★ If you could move any of the planets or the sun, where would you move them to?

BLOCK 3:3

Theme: **WEATHER**

Strand: **EXPRESS**

The Weather theme is the vehicle to the Express Jellyfish strand. Express invites us to explore the possibilities of our imagination, our thoughts and our feelings. Weather has the potential to reflect so many human traits and can provide us with a powerful metaphor in which to express ourselves.

Initial gathering: brushing off/Jellyfish breathing/Jellyfish wave

Exploring the theme: choose from...

Task	**Bodywork**
Share and then display large images of different kinds of weather around the room. Call out a range of different emotions and for each one ask the children to choose which weather image they instinctively feel it relates to. They can do this by standing by the image – the Jellyfish teacher should model this first. Ask volunteers to share their thoughts on their choice. Repeat for different emotions – you could use the **Jellyfish picture cards** (B1:1) for ideas.	★ Raindrop ★ Lightning ★ Sun ★ Snowflake ★ Tornado
Massage	**Visualization**
★ **Permission, hug and frame** ★ Sun ★ Cloud ★ Lightning ★ Tornado ★ Rain ★ **Personal signature and hug**	**See Weather visualization**

Creative expression: to support children to recognize and express feelings, you may like to:

- Provide a **weather diary template**
- Invite children to create a weather picture
- Allow free choice

Final gathering: Jellyfish gallery

Questions to support creative chatter:

On the shore

- What has the weather been like?
- What activity would someone feel like doing on a weather day like this?
- What could make this weather change?

Under the sea

- What sound would this weather make?
- How would this weather make people feel?
- How might this weather make someone behave?

BLOCK 3:4

Theme: SECRET GARDEN

Strand: MANAGE

The Secret Garden theme is the vehicle to the Manage Jellyfish strand. Manage helps us to acknowledge thoughts, feelings and situations safely. The notion of a secret garden is one that allows for security. The garden and its contents are known only by those we wish to let in. It can safely contain thoughts, feelings, relationships and events within the confines of the space, as well as providing us with room to grow.

Initial gathering: brushing off/Jellyfish breathing/Jellyfish wave

Exploring the theme: choose from…

Task	**Bodywork**
Provide children with a small plant pot (alternatively a yogurt pot/cardboard egg box cups would be perfect). Give each child a bean and ask them to hold it tightly in their hands. As they do so, children should think of a positive emotion, feeling or behaviour that is poignant to them. The bean should then be planted in the pot with soil. Ensure children understand that now we have planted the emotion it cannot be seen but it is still there; it needs caring for to help it grow.	★ Seed ★ Grow one ★ Grow two ★ Grow three ★ Bloom
Massage	**Visualization**
★ **Permission, hug and frame** ★ Sunshine and rain ★ Stems ★ Leaves ★ Buds ★ Flowers ★ **Personal signature and hug**	**See Secret Garden visualization**

Creative expression: to support children to create a space to manage and grow thoughts, feelings, relationships and events, you may like to:

- Provide the **keyhole template** that leads to a secret garden
- Invite children to create their own secret garden
- Allow free choice

Final gathering: Jellyfish gallery

Questions to support creative chatter:

On the shore

- Whose secret garden is through this keyhole?
- What grows in this secret garden?
- Who looks after this secret garden?

Under the sea

- If something could be removed from this secret garden, what might it be?
- If something extra could be added to this secret garden, what might it be?
- What do you think makes this garden secret?

BLOCK 3:5

Theme:
MIRRORS AND MASKS

Strand:
DEVELOP

The Mirrors and Masks theme is the vehicle to the Develop Jellyfish strand. Develop helps us to grow as individuals, in our relationships and in our lives. It helps us to explore possibilities, move forwards and make changes for the better. Mirrors and Masks explores the possibilities of what we see and what we allow others to see, giving us the confidence to develop and work with our many masks.

Initial gathering: brushing off/Jellyfish breathing/Jellyfish wave

Exploring the theme: choose from…

Task	Bodywork
Invite each child to choose a mask and spend some time looking at themselves in a mirror while wearing it. Ask children to say 'Hello' to the group, speaking as the mask. Now invite the group to move round the space in character greeting one another, using a persona that suits the mask. Next ask them to change masks with the person closest to them and repeat the meet-and-greet activity. Once the activity is over, instruct everyone to remove their masks and invite them to share who they met and their experiences of wearing the masks. Was the experience different with each mask?	★ Mirror one ★ Mirror two ★ Mirror three ★ Mirror four ★ Mask
Massage	**Visualization**
★ **Permission, hug and frame** ★ Create a mirror ★ Draw a face in the reflection ★ Draw three different expressions on the face, e.g. excited, angry, scared, shocked, sad, laughing, calm, thoughtful ★ **Personal signature and hug**	**See Mirrors and Masks visualization**

Creative expression: to support children to develop an understanding of self and those around them, you may like to:

- ★ Provide the **mirror template** to draw a helpful face
- ★ Invite children to make a mask to paint/decorate
- ★ Allow free choice

Final gathering: Jellyfish gallery

Questions to support creative chatter:

On the shore

- ★ What does this reflection show?
- ★ What is special about this reflection?
- ★ If you could, what would you like to change about this reflection?

Under the sea

- ★ How does it feel to see this reflection?
- ★ What might this reflection be thinking?
- ★ What will this reflection be able to achieve?

BLOCK 3: RESOURCES

Theme	Task	Bodywork	Massage	Visualization	Creative expression
Animals	What am I? cards	Animals	As listed on class plans	Animals	Animal images or figures
Deep Space	Planet template	Deep Space		Deep Space	Solar system template Clay
Weather	Images of different weather Jellyfish picture cards (B1:1)	Weather		Weather	Weather diary template
Secret Garden	Soil Pot Beans	Secret Garden		Secret Garden	Keyhole template
Mirrors and Masks	Variety of masks Mirror	Mirrors and Masks		Mirrors and Masks	Mirror template Blank masks

Highlighted items are provided in this book: resources are at the end of this block, massage suggestions are included in the class plans, and bodywork illustrations and visualization outlines are listed at the end of the book.

ANIMALS B3:1 WHAT AM I? CARDS

I am large and people say I am the King. You wouldn't want to stroke me as I have a very large bite!

Who am I?

A lion

I like to eat grass. Some people say I look like a cloud. My coat will definitely keep you warm!

Who am I?

A sheep

I don't have any arms or legs. Sometimes I hiss but mostly I like to wrap myself around you!

Who am I?

A snake

I listen well but find it hard to see. I love to go out at night and you'll find me sleeping upside down!

Who am I?

A bat

I have two legs and like to watch you from a tree. You might have heard me t'wit or t'woo!

Who am I?

An owl

I have large ears and love to hop. I'm soft and everybody loves my cute tail!

Who am I?

A rabbit

People say that I am cheeky. I have long arms and legs and my tail is truly excellent for swinging!

Who am I?

A monkey

I live in the sea and have great sharp teeth. I look smooth to touch and I am silent and swift!

Who am I?

A shark

I live in the mountains and in the snow. I can be black, brown or white.

Who am I?

A bear

I'm clever and I perch on high places. I bring you gifts to show you I love you!

Who am I?

A cat

I swim and I walk, I clap and I talk. Come and watch me entertain you!

Who am I?

A sea lion

I am too tall for you to see but I am always fluttering my eyelashes at you!

Who am I?

A giraffe

I'm a large mammal, only the ocean can hold me and only the ocean can hide me!

Who am I?

An whale

I can be wild and free or yours to keep. I love it when you plait my hair and brush my coat!

Who am I?

A horse

I fly and I work non-stop but I never get any thanks. I bring a treat to your breakfast table!

Who am I?

A bee

I sing with my wings and I love sweet things. I'm hard to spot but listen closely to find me!

Who am I?

A humming bird

DEEP SPACE B3:2 PLANET TEMPLATE

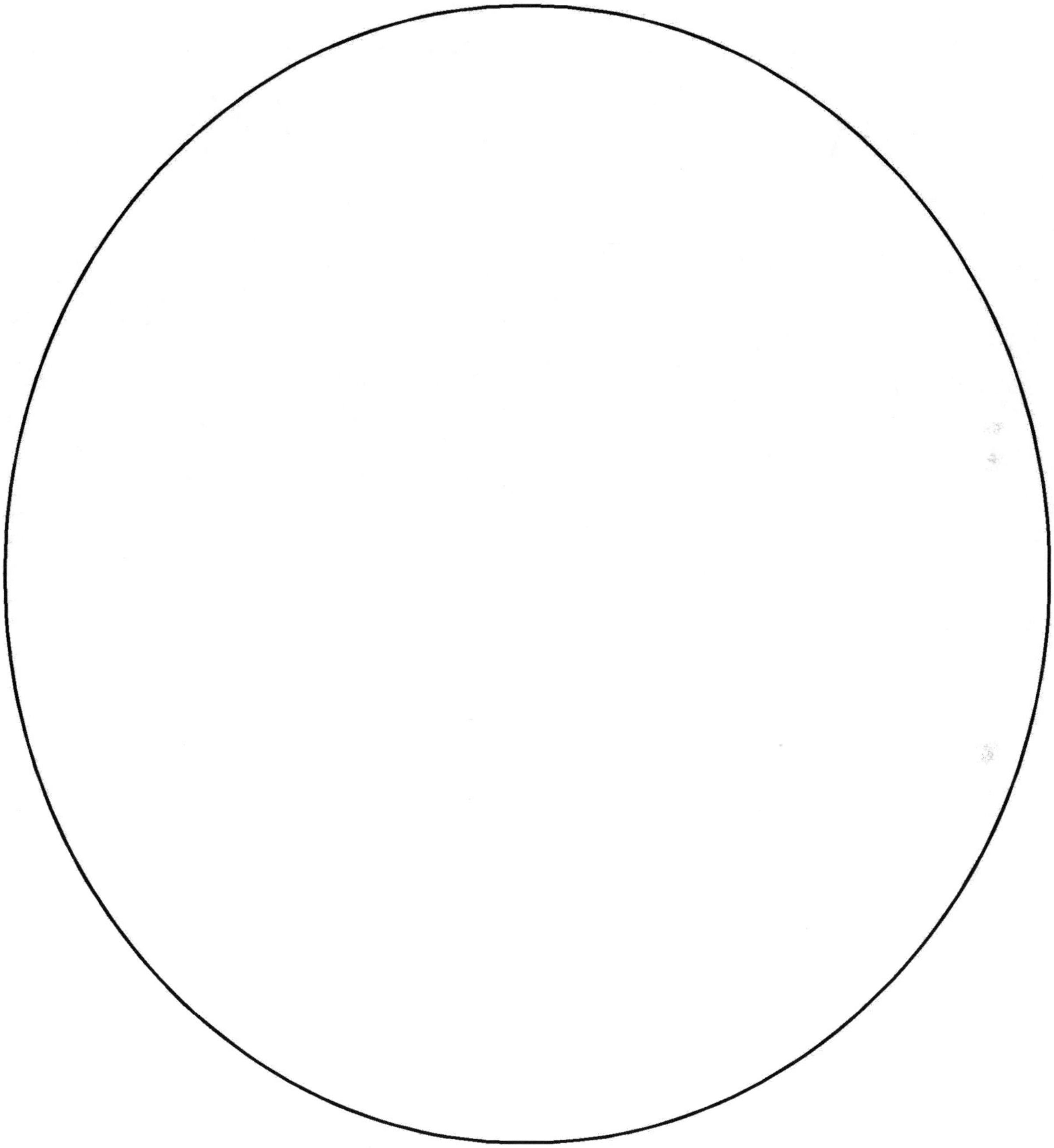

DEEP SPACE B3:2 SOLAR SYSTEM TEMPLATE

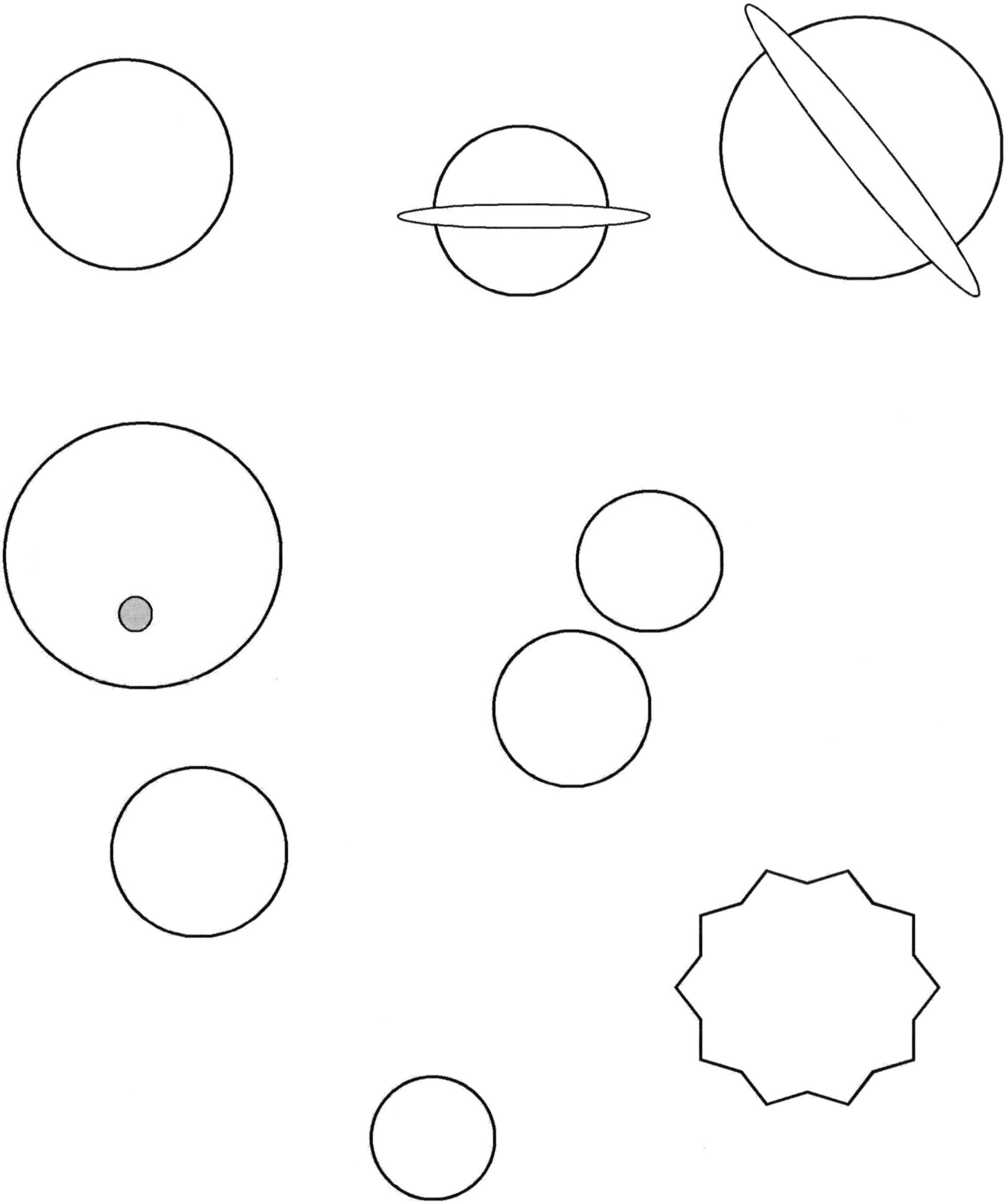

WEATHER B3:3 WEATHER DIARY TEMPLATE

Today is....	The weather today is....
Monday	
Tuesday	
Wednesday	
Thursday	
Friday	

SECRET GARDEN B3:4 KEYHOLE TEMPLATE

MIRRORS AND MASKS B3:5
MIRROR TEMPLATE

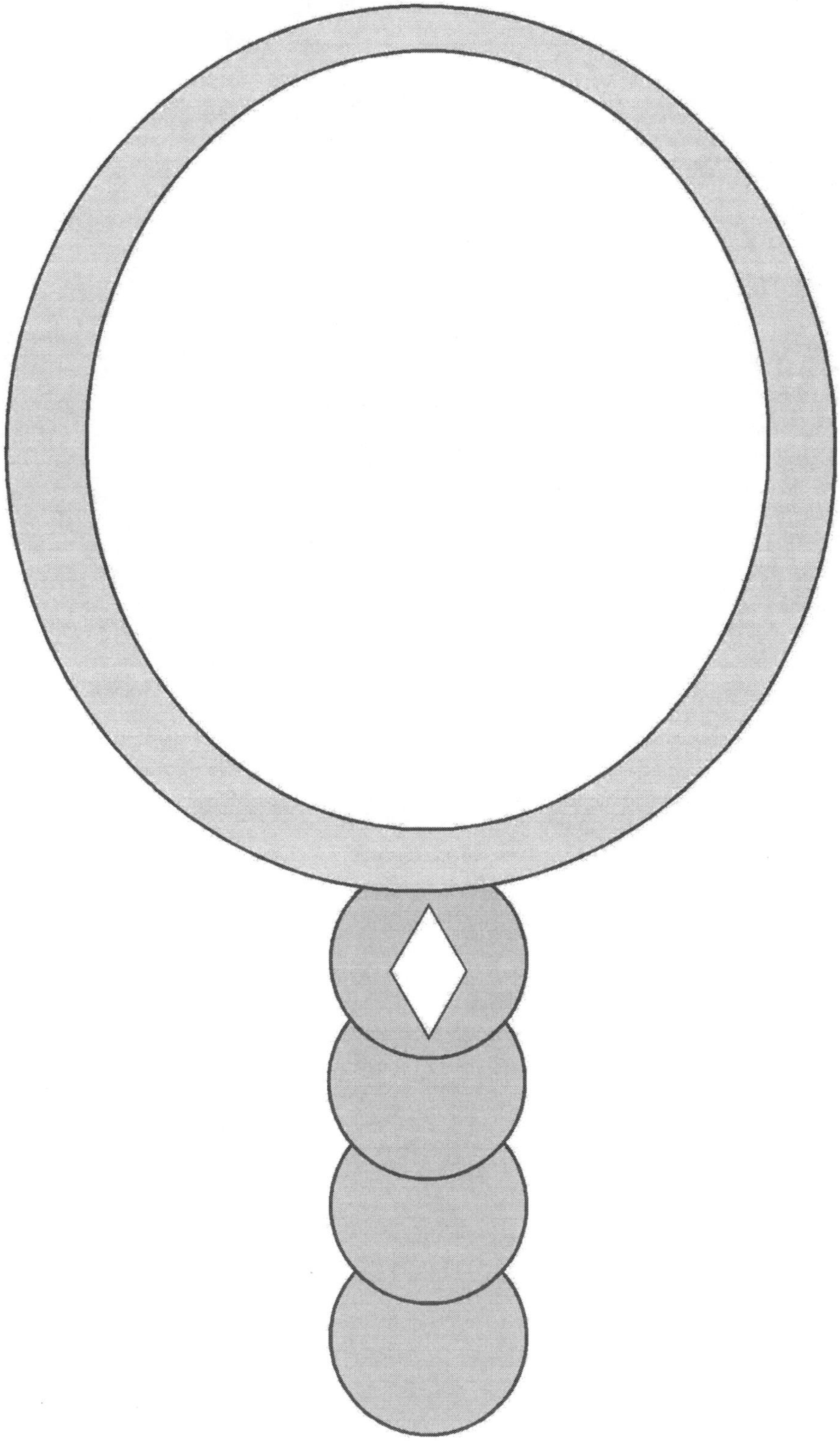

Block 4

CLASS PLANS AND RESOURCES

BLOCK 4:1

Theme: **CIRCUS**

Strand: **DISCOVER**

The Circus theme is the vehicle for the Discover Jellyfish strand and so enables us to safely discover how we see ourselves, relationships with others and the world around us. At the circus you can discover all sorts of weird and wonderful performers, each with their own unique talent.

Initial gathering: brushing off/Jellyfish breathing/Jellyfish wave

Exploring the theme: choose from...

Task	**Bodywork**
Ask the children to choose a performer from the list of **circus performers** provided. Once each child has chosen an act, invite them to create a circus flyer from the **flyer template** to promote their performer. For older children flyers should include three statements about the performer. It is fine for children to choose the same acts/performers as others, as their interpretation of them will still be individual. Invite children to talk about their flyer either by sharing it with the group or in pairs. Ask them to focus on why they have chosen that act.	★ Ringmaster ★ Strongman ★ Tightrope walker ★ Juggler ★ Unicyclist
Massage	**Visualization**
★ **Permission, hug and frame** ★ Circus ring ★ Trapeze artist swinging ★ Tightrope walker ★ Juggling balls ★ Round of applause ★ **Personal signature and hug**	**See Circus visualization**

Creative expression: to support children to discover their own talents and qualities, you may like to:

- ★ Provide a circus **tent template**
- ★ Invite the children to create a circus
- ★ Allow free choice

Final gathering: Jellyfish gallery

Questions to support creative chatter:

On the shore

- ★ Who is performing in this circus?
- ★ Which is your favourite act?
- ★ Which is your least favourite act?

Under the sea

- ★ How do the performers feel about their circus acts?
- ★ If you were a circus performer, what act would you like to be?
- ★ How might it feel to perform an act to a circus crowd?

BLOCK 4:2

Theme: **DESERTS** Strand: **EXPLORE**

The Deserts theme is the vehicle to the Explore Jellyfish strand. Through Explore we seek to find out more about what we have discovered and hope to gain a greater understanding and appreciation of who we are. Deserts are dry, barren places and yet when we look closer, there is a lot more to them; we just have to look.

Initial gathering: brushing off/Jellyfish breathing/Jellyfish wave

Exploring the theme: choose from…

Task	**Bodywork**
Provide a small sand tray/s. Invite the children to explore the sand using their hands and fingers – to do whatever comes naturally. This could be impressions, movement, pattern making, etc. Ensure quiet music is playing and encourage silence and focus on the sand. Children may wish to do this in pairs or, if resources allow, individually. Allow between 5 and 15 minutes but use your judgement on how long you think they need. Extend this task by inviting children to create a desert scene forming dunes and adding objects. Allow time for the children to talk about the contents of their tray.	★ Dune ★ Cactus ★ Meerkat ★ Camel ★ Snake
Massage	**Visualization**
★ **Permission, hug and frame** ★ Sand dunes ★ Cracks in the earth ★ Desert snake ★ Camel footprints ★ Lizard feet ★ **Personal signature and hug**	**See Deserts visualization**

Creative expression: to support children to explore their environment, you may like to:

- ★ Provide children with a **dunes template**
- ★ Invite the children to create a desert landscape or desert-dwelling creature
- ★ Allow free choice

Final gathering: Jellyfish gallery

Questions to support creative chatter:

On the shore

- ★ Where is this desert?
- ★ Is it easy or difficult to reach?
- ★ Who or what is in this desert?

Under the sea

- ★ Which feature in this desert are you most drawn to and why?
- ★ How might it feel to be in this desert?
- ★ What could be hidden beneath the sands of this desert?

BLOCK 4:3

Theme: HATS AND HEADDRESSES

Strand: EXPRESS

The Hats and Headdresses theme is the vehicle to the Express Jellyfish strand. Express invites us to explore the possibilities of our imagination, our thoughts and our feelings. Wearing a hat or a headdress can completely alter how we feel and behave. We can take on different roles, personas and attitudes. Through hats and headdresses we can endeavour to express a little more of who we are or who we would like to be.

Initial gathering: brushing off/Jellyfish breathing/Jellyfish wave

Exploring the theme: choose from...

Task	Bodywork
Using the **hat cards** ask the children: ★ Who would wear this hat? ★ How would it feel to wear a hat like this? ★ What qualities would the hat wearer have? Allow for discussion and repeat for different **hat cards**. Alternatively, you could ask for volunteers within the group to wear some different hats/headdresses and act out the character of the wearer. Remember there is no right or wrong answer to how the different hats/headdresses make people feel.	★ Top hat ★ Feather headdress ★ Bonnet ★ Turban ★ Crown
Massage	**Visualization**
★ **Permission, hug and frame** ★ A wizard's hat ★ A feathered headdress ★ A sun hat ★ A tiara ★ A bobble hat ★ **Personal signature and hug**	**See Hats and Headdresses visualization**

Creative expression: to support children to express who they are or would like to be, you may like to:

- ★ Provide **hat templates**
- ★ Invite the children to create their own hat or headdress
- ★ Allow free choice

Final gathering: Jellyfish gallery

Questions to support creative chatter:

On the shore

- ★ Who might this hat/headdress belong to?
- ★ How would someone feel wearing this hat/headdress?
- ★ Where could this hat/headdress be worn?

Under the sea

- ★ Which qualities would the hat/headdress wearer have?
- ★ How would someone wearing a hat/headdress like this behave?
- ★ What things might the hat/headdress wearer be able to do?

BLOCK 4:4

Theme: POCKETS

Strand: MANAGE

The Pocket theme is the vehicle to the Manage Jellyfish strand. Manage helps us to acknowledge thoughts, feelings and situations safely. Pockets are handy places to keep things like keys and money safe. A pocket is therefore the perfect place to keep anything that we wish to keep secure. They can also be places to store the things we need or a place to keep things hidden.

Initial gathering: brushing off/Jellyfish breathing/Jellyfish wave

Exploring the theme: choose from…

Task	Bodywork
You will need either an item of clothing with a pocket or a cut-out pocket from an old piece of clothing. Inside the pocket you should have prepared the **pocket words** provided. These words are examples of emotions, feelings and behaviours that could be kept in a pocket. Ask the group what sort of things we keep in pockets and why. What could be in this pocket? Invite children to remove and share words from the pocket and together discuss why they may be in there.	★ Fabric ★ Scissors ★ Needle ★ Stitch ★ Pocket
Massage	**Visualization**
★ **Permission, hug and frame** ★ Cut the shape ★ Stitch the pocket ★ How does the pocket open? Zip, button… ★ How deep is the pocket? ★ Fasten the pocket closed ★ **Personal signature and hug**	**See Pockets visualization**

Creative expression: to support children to manage thoughts, feelings and behaviours, you may like to:

- ★ Provide a **pocket template**
- ★ Invite the children to make their own pocket from a material such as felt
- ★ Allow free choice

Final gathering: Jellyfish gallery

Questions to support creative chatter:

On the shore

- ★ Whose pocket is this?
- ★ What is in this pocket?
- ★ How could this pocket be secured?

Under the sea

- ★ Why are there items in this pocket? (If the pocket is empty, why is it empty?)
- ★ How can the items in this pocket be used?
- ★ What could be added to this pocket and why?

BLOCK 4:5

Theme: **FOOTPRINTS**

Strand: **DEVELOP**

The Footprints theme is the vehicle to the Develop Jellyfish strand. Develop helps us to grow as individuals, in our relationships and in our lives. It helps us to explore possibilities and move forwards and make changes for the better. As footprints map and record the direction we are moving in they are ideal for helping us to move forward in our own lives.

Initial gathering: brushing off/Jellyfish breathing/Jellyfish wave

Exploring the theme: choose from…

Task	Bodywork
Ask children to choose a colouring pencil and a coloured piece. Model drawing the outline of your foot. Now invite the group to do the same. Some children may find it easier to do this in pairs. Once everyone has an outline of their foot, instruct them to write or draw anything that they feel may be helpful on their life journey. Discuss ideas if necessary. The paper feet should then be cut out and placed on or around the **focal point**.	★ Print 1 ★ Print 2 ★ March print ★ Heel toe print ★ Side rocking print
Massage	**Visualization**
★ **Permission, hug and frame** ★ A foot ★ Big footsteps ★ Little footsteps ★ Quick footsteps ★ Careful footsteps ★ **Personal signature and hug**	**See Footprints visualization**

Creative expression: to support children to develop their own path, you may like to:

- ★ Provide **footprints templates**
- ★ Invite the children to record their footprint using paint, dough or clay
- ★ Allow free choice

Final gathering: Jellyfish gallery

Questions to support creative chatter:

On the shore

- ★ Whose footprints could these be?
- ★ Which direction are these footprints travelling in?
- ★ Where do you think these footprints could be going?

Under the sea

- ★ How do these footprints feel about the destination to which they are going?
- ★ What is helping these footprints on their journey?
- ★ What do you think about where the footprints are going?

BLOCK 4: RESOURCES

Theme	Task	Bodywork	Massage	Visualization	Creative expression
Circus	Circus performers Flyer template	Circus	As listed on class plans	Circus	Tent template
Deserts	Sand trays and sand	Deserts		Deserts	Dunes template
Hats and Head-dresses	Hat cards	Hats and Head-dresses		Hats and Headdresses	Hat templates
Pockets	Pocket Pocket words	Pockets		Pockets	Pocket template Felt Needles and thread
Footprints	Coloured pens and paper	Footprints		Footprints	Footprints templates Paint, dough or clay

Highlighted items are provided in this book: resources are at the end of this block, massage suggestions are included in the class plans, and bodywork illustrations and visualization outlines are listed at the end of the book.

CIRCUS B4:1 CIRCUS PERFORMERS

Acrobat
Animal trainer
Clown
Dancer
Fire artist
Fortune teller

Hula hooper

Human cannon ball

Juggler

Lion tamer

Knife thrower

Mime artist

Magician
Plate spinner
Puppet master
Ringmaster
Stilt walker
Strongman

Tightrope walker

Trapeze artist

Trick rider

Unicyclist

CIRCUS B4:1 FLYER TEMPLATE

Circus

CIRCUS B4:1 TENT TEMPLATE

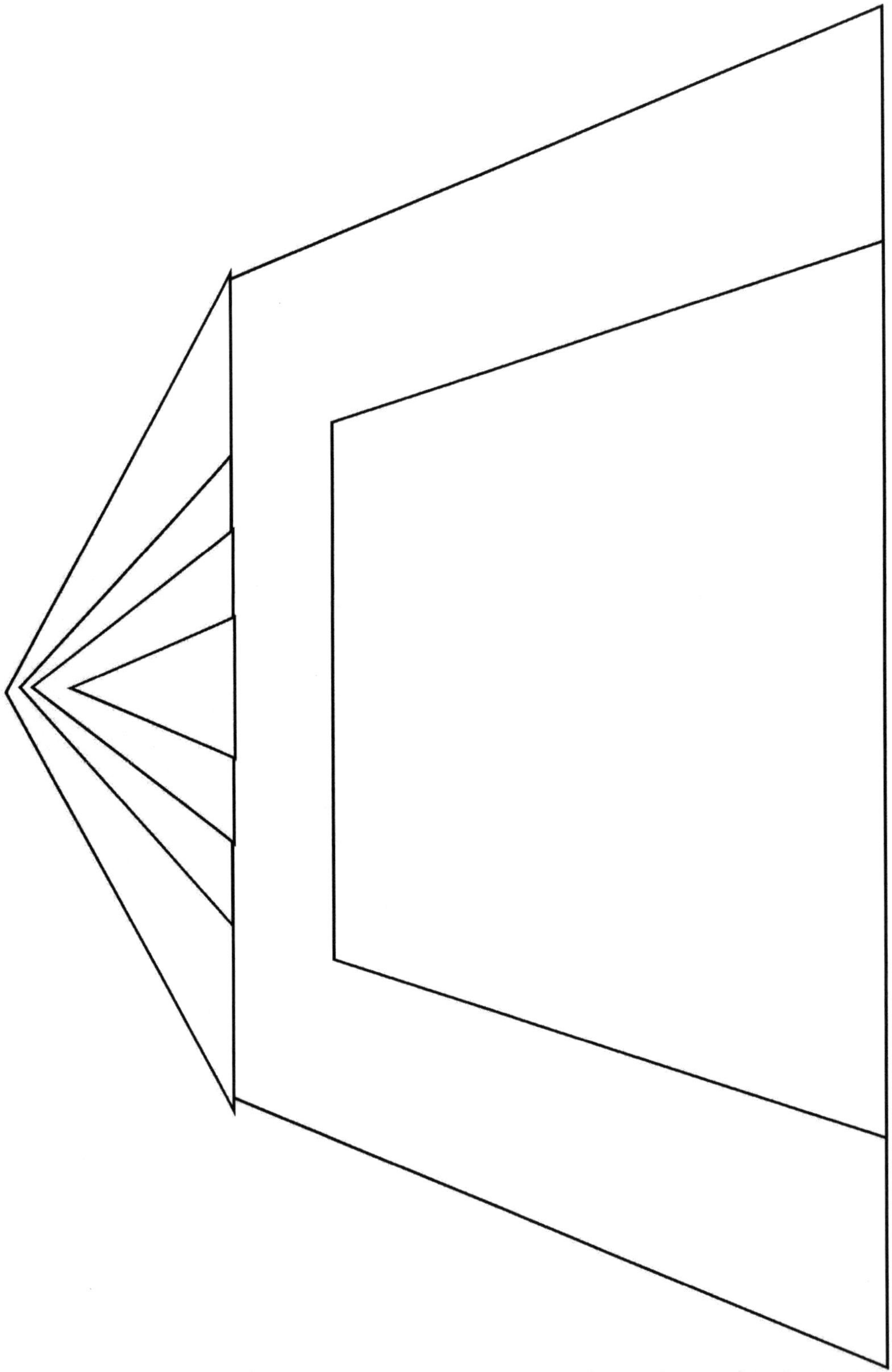

DESERTS B4:2 DUNES TEMPLATE

HATS AND HEADDRESSES B4:3 HAT CARDS

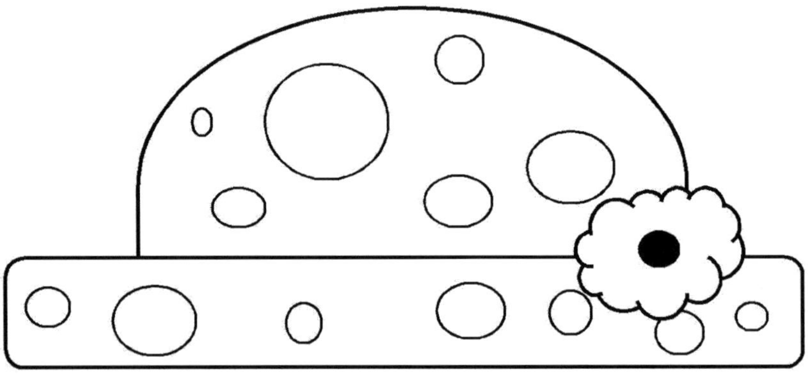

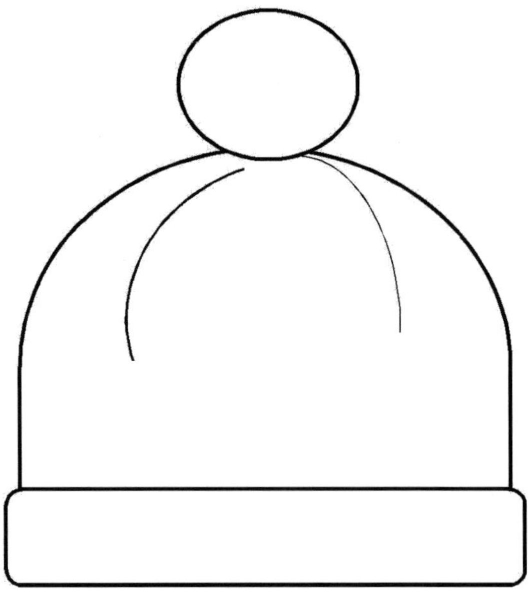

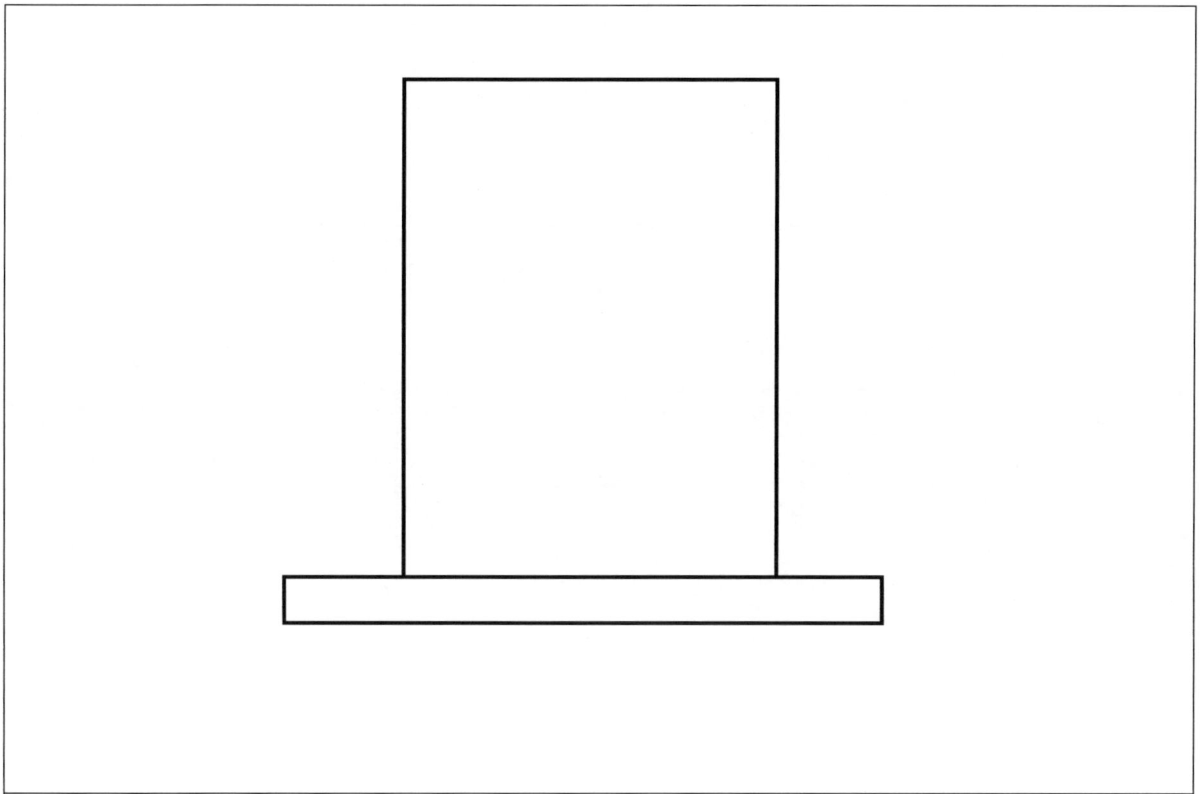

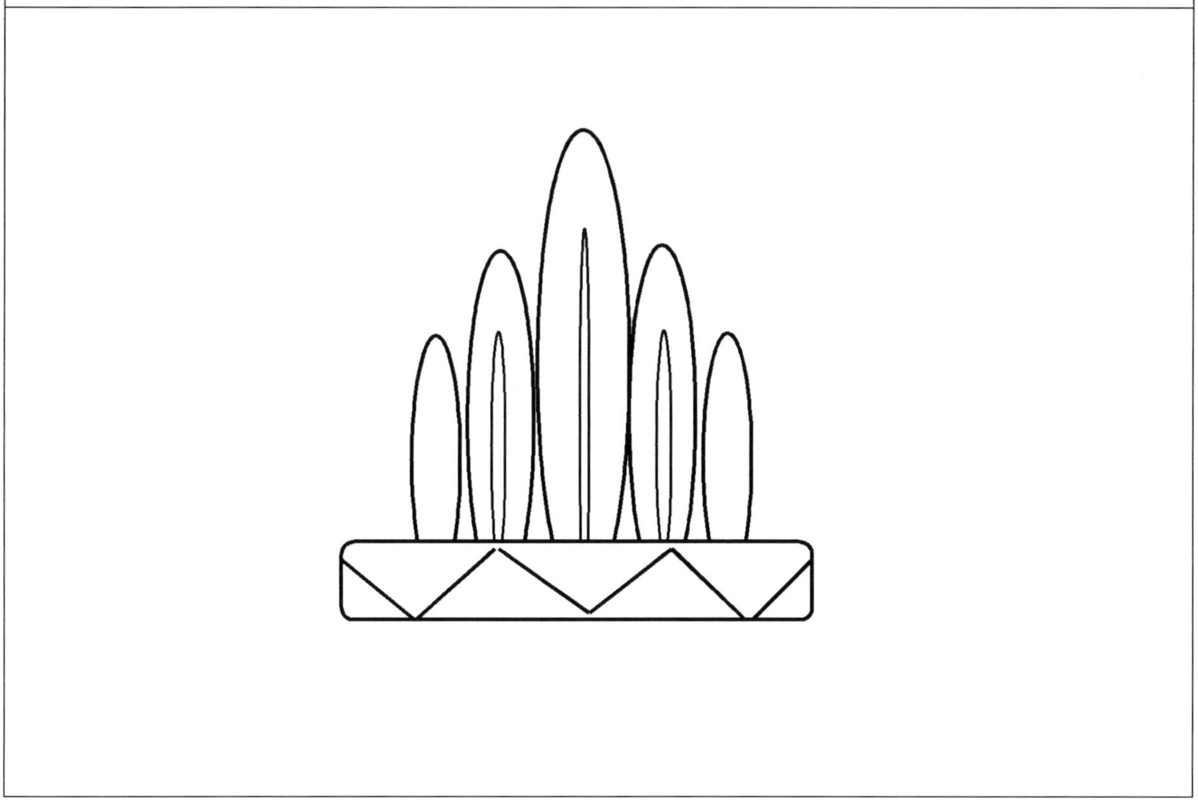

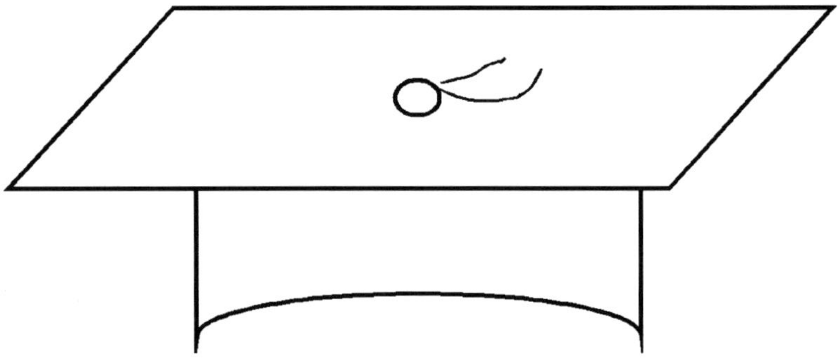

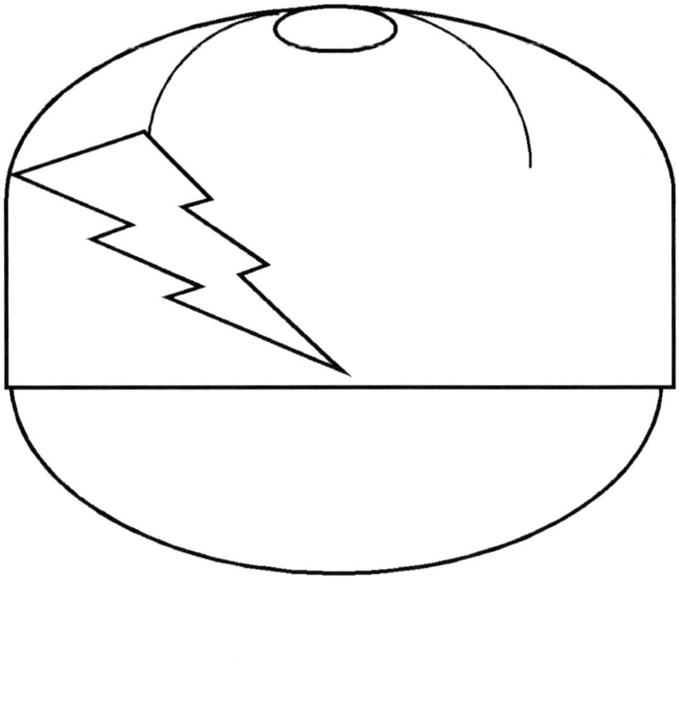

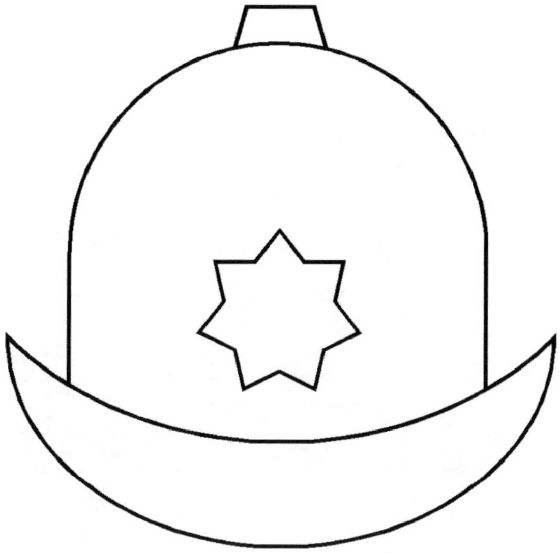

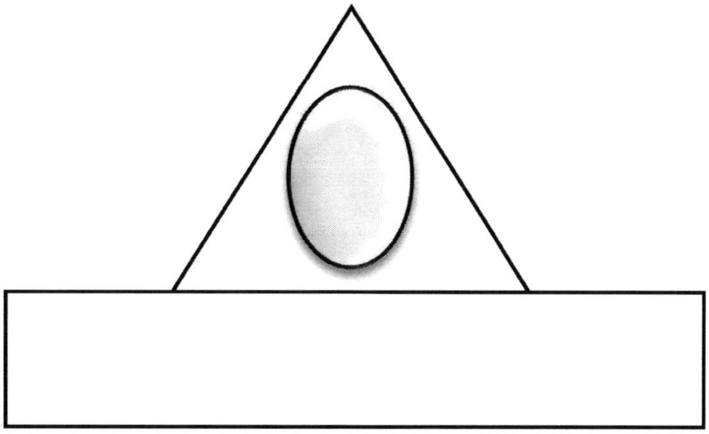

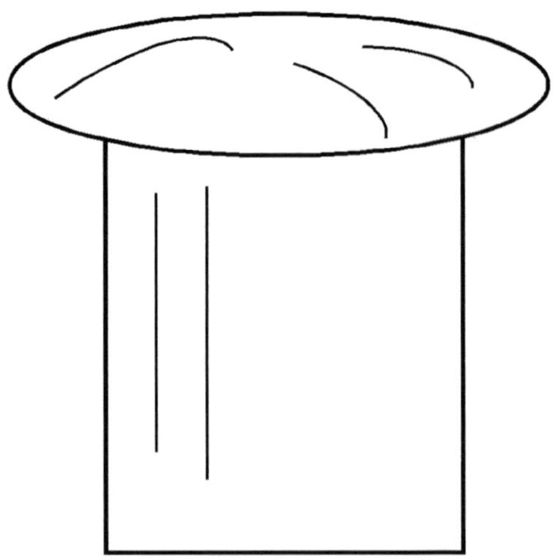

HATS AND HEADDRESSES
B4:3 HAT TEMPLATES

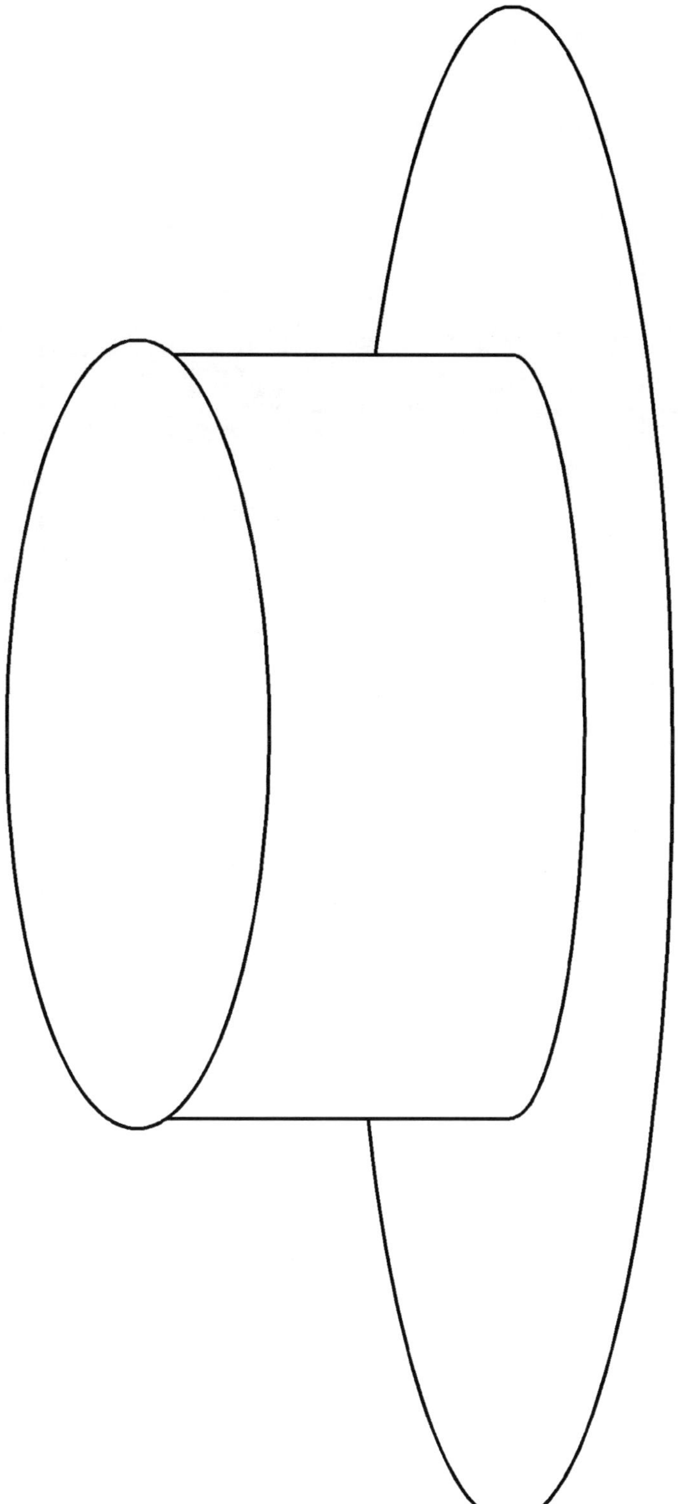

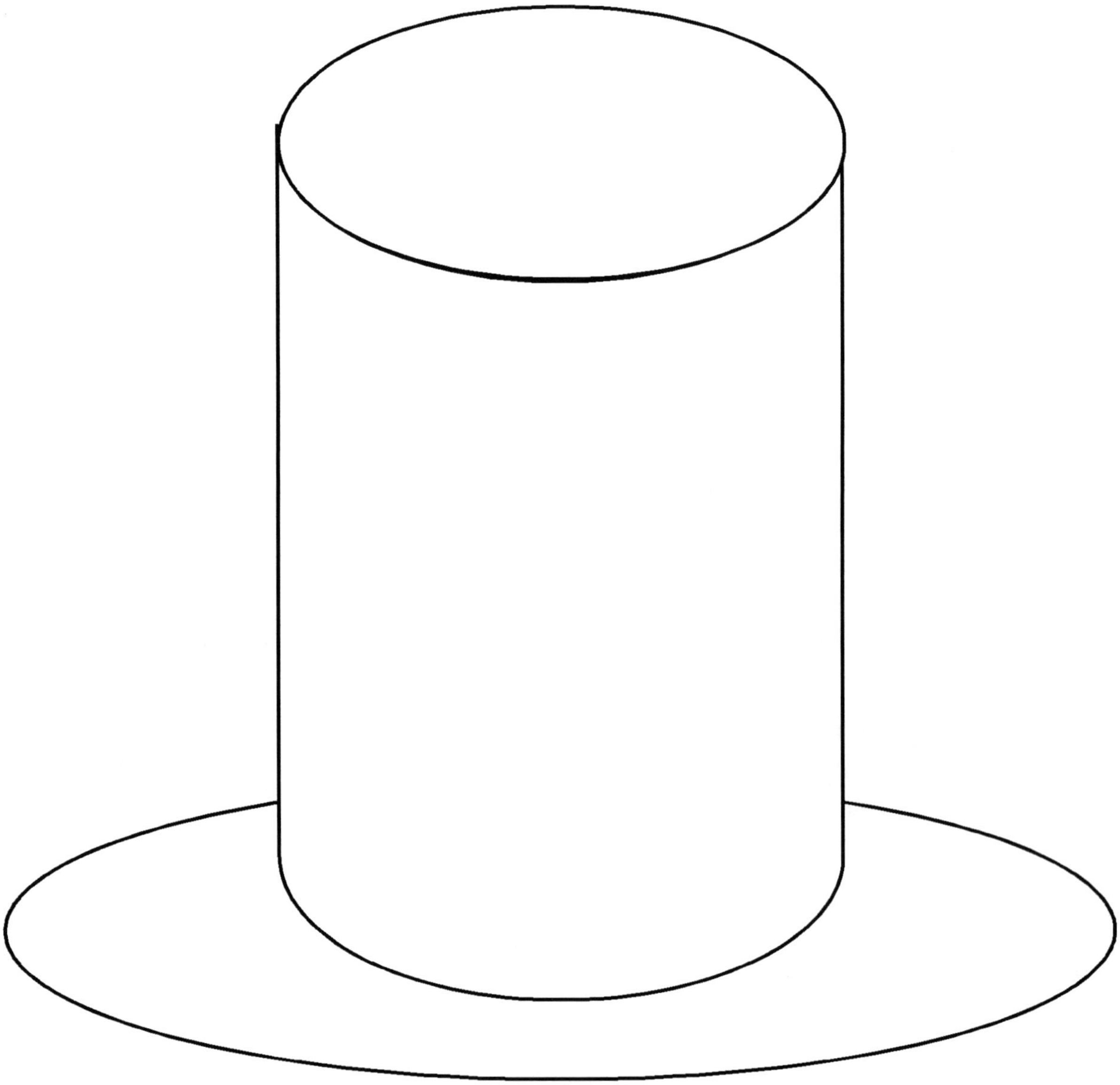

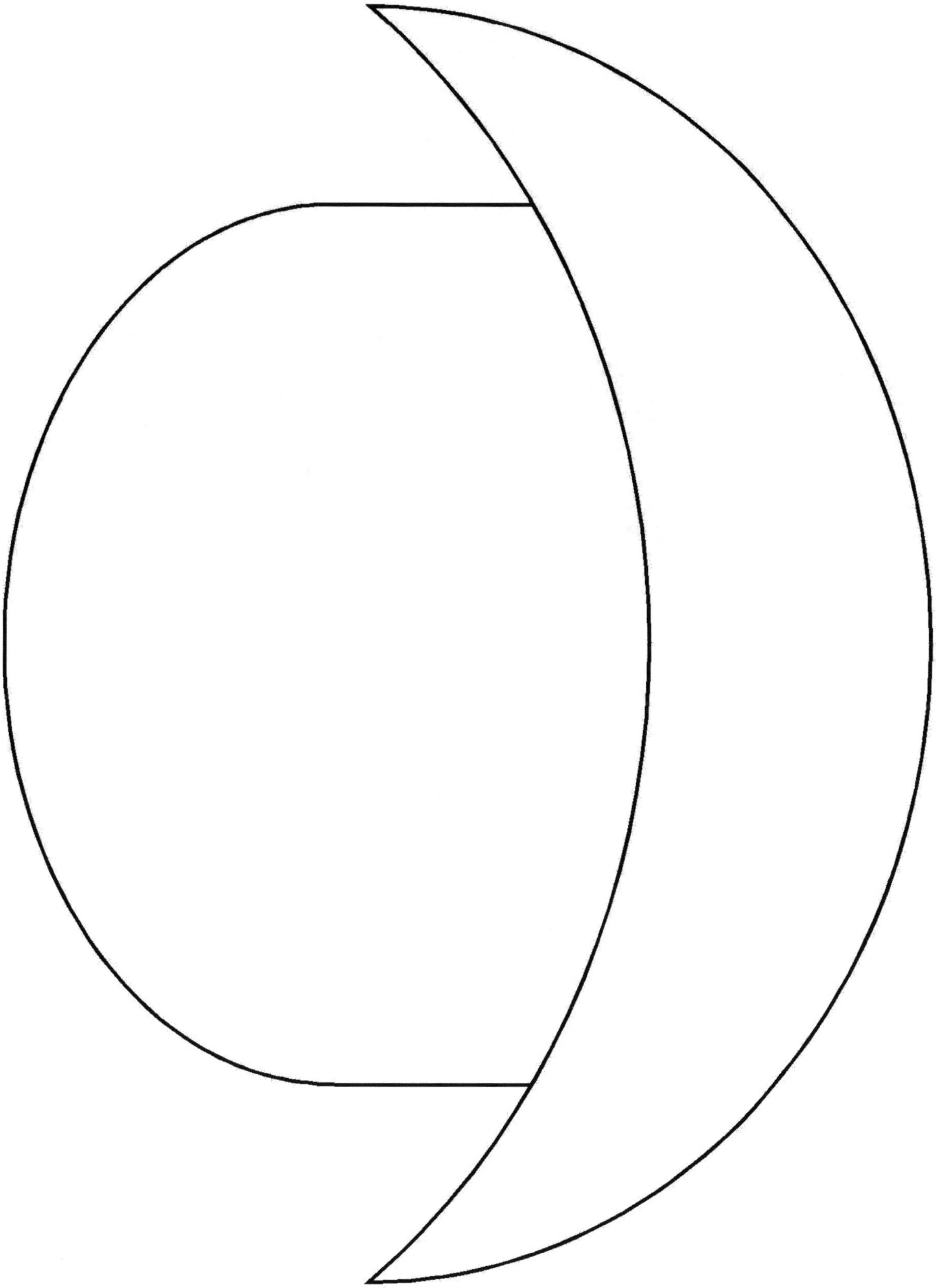

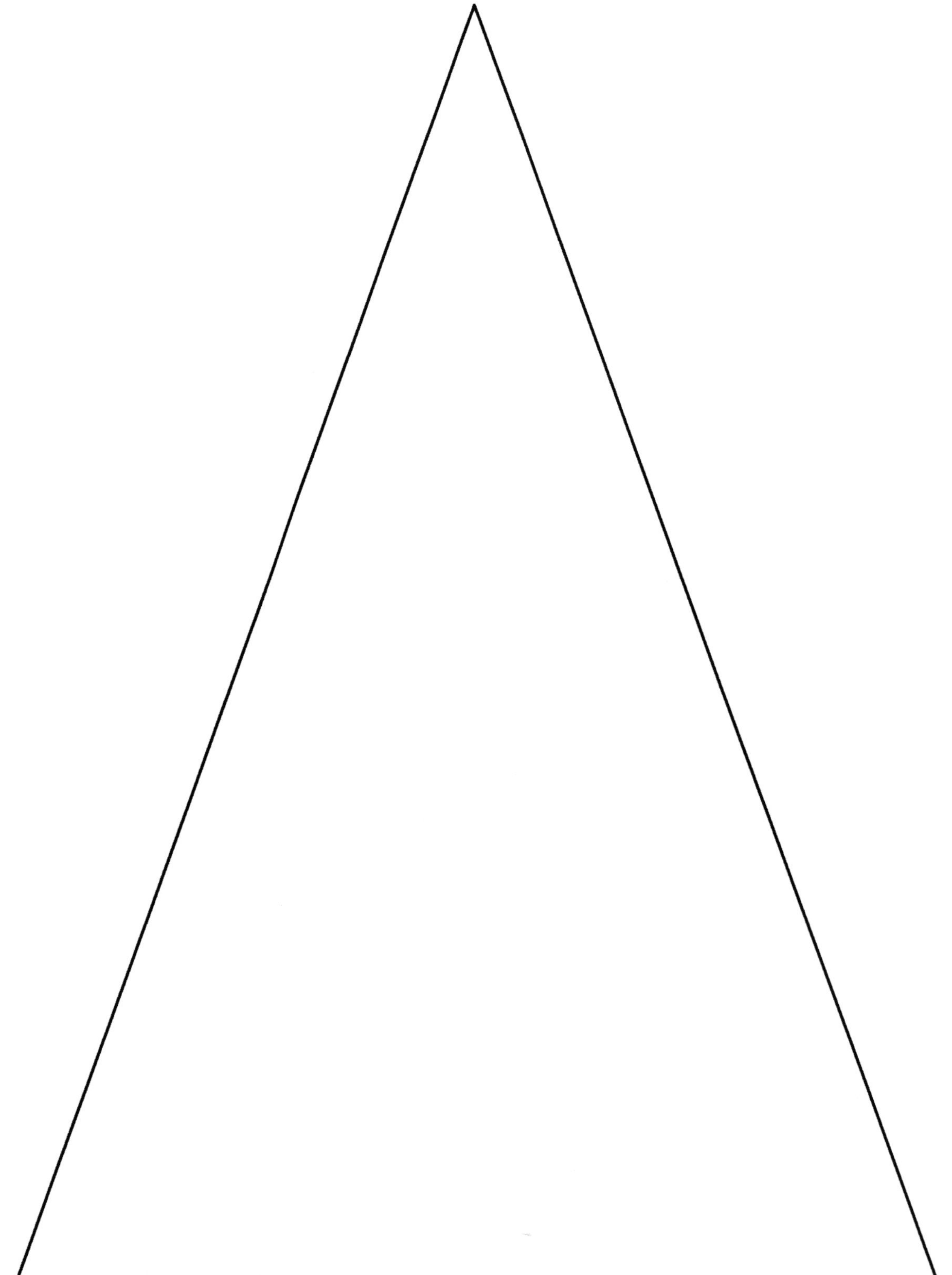

POCKETS B4:4 POCKET WORDS

Anger

Confidence

Fear

Wisdom

Strength

Panic

Knowledge

Love

Understanding

POCKETS B4:4 POCKET TEMPLATE

FOOTPRINTS B4:5 FOOTPRINTS TEMPLATES

Block 5

CLASS PLANS AND RESOURCES

BLOCK 5:1

Theme: BOOKS

Strand: DISCOVER

The Books theme is the vehicle for the Discover Jellyfish strand and so enables us to safely discover how we see ourselves, relationships with others and the world around us. Books can be both real and imaginary, with settings and plots only limited by our imagination. The Books theme can help us to discover our own stories, where they are set, who the characters are, what the plots are and how they play out.

Initial gathering: brushing off/Jellyfish breathing/Jellyfish wave

Exploring the theme: choose from…

Task	Bodywork
Cover a children's story book in paper. Show the children the wrapped book and tell them it is a story book but do not reveal the title. Ask the group the following questions: ★ What could the story be? ★ Where could the story be set? ★ Who might the characters be? ★ What could happen to the characters? Share and discuss ideas together. Reveal the wrapped book at the end of the task.	★ Closed book ★ Open book ★ Reader 1 ★ Reader 2 ★ Reader 3
Massage	**Visualization**
★ **Permission, hug and frame** ★ Outline of the book ★ Run fingers over the cover ★ Trace the letters, shapes and patterns ★ Turn the pages ★ Close the book ★ **Personal signature and hug**	**See Books visualization**

Creative expression: to support children to discover some of their own stories, you may like to:

- ★ Provide the **book cover template**
- ★ Invite the children to create their own story book
- ★ Allow free choice

Final gathering: Jellyfish gallery

Questions to support creative chatter:

On the shore

- ★ Is this book imaginary or real?
- ★ Where is this book set?
- ★ What is this book about?

Under the sea

- ★ What are the characters in this book like?
- ★ What might other people think about this book?
- ★ Who might be interested in reading this book?

BLOCK 5:2

Theme: **HOT AIR BALLOONS**

Strand: **EXPLORE**

The Hot Air Balloons theme is the vehicle to the Explore Jellyfish strand. Through Explore we seek to find out more about what we have discovered and hope to gain a greater understanding and appreciation of who we are. A balloon ride can gently take us in a number of directions. Just pick a balloon and off you go.

Initial gathering: brushing off/Jellyfish breathing/Jellyfish wave

Exploring the theme: choose from...

Task	**Bodywork**
Prepare enough balloons in a variety of colours for the children in your group. Stand each balloon in its own cup to mimic a hot air balloon. Invite each child to select a balloon, reminding them to handle it carefully. Tell the children their balloon can travel anywhere they want it to go. Share ideas and discuss possibilities; destinations can be real or imaginary. Ask the children to decide upon a destination for their balloon before handing them a marker pen in which to write or draw where they want the balloon to go. Children may share where their balloon is headed and how it would feel to be there.	★ Basket ★ Strings ★ Balloon ★ Take off ★ Fly away
Massage	**Visualization**
★ **Permission, hug and frame** ★ Weave the basket ★ Create the balloon ★ Tie the ropes ★ Light the fire ★ Fly away ★ **Personal signature and hug**	**See Hot Air Balloons visualization**

Creative expression: to support children to explore the places they would like to go, you may like to:

- ★ Provide the **hot air balloon template**
- ★ Invite children to create a scene for their hot air balloon destination
- ★ Allow free choice

Final gathering: Jellyfish gallery

Questions to support creative chatter:

On the shore

- ★ Where has this balloon come from?
- ★ Where is this balloon journeying to?
- ★ How might it feel to take a ride in this hot air balloon?

Under the sea

- ★ What things has this balloon seen on its journey?
- ★ What will this balloon see when it reaches its destination?
- ★ How does this balloon feel about its journey?

BLOCK 5:3

Theme: TEXTURES

Strand: EXPRESS

The Textures theme is the vehicle to the Express Jellyfish strand. Express invites us to explore the possibilities of our imagination, our thoughts and our feelings. Through textures we can express and experiment with feelings and emotions in a tactile way. We securely experience different sensations and the effect they have on us.

Initial gathering: brushing off/Jellyfish breathing/Jellyfish wave

Exploring the theme: choose from...

Task	**Bodywork**
Prepare a bag containing a number of materials of different textures. Sitting in the **gathering place** pass the bag around the circle of children and ask them to close their eyes as they place their hands into the bag. Encourage everyone to feel the different textures and describe them, including how they make them feel.	★ Smooth touch ★ Spiky touch ★ Bumpy touch ★ Rough touch ★ Fluffy touch
Massage	**Visualization**
★ **Permission, hug and frame** ★ Bumpy ★ Smooth ★ Rough ★ Ridged ★ Rippled ★ **Personal signature and hug**	**See Textures visualization**

Creative expression: to support children to express their feelings and emotions, you may like to:

- ★ Provide the **patchwork template**
- ★ Invite children to make their own book of textures using techniques such as crayon rubbing, embossing metal foil and making marks in dough
- ★ Allow free choice

Final gathering: Jellyfish gallery

Questions to support creative chatter:

On the shore

- ★ Which textures can you see?
- ★ Which is your favourite texture and why?
- ★ Which is your least favourite texture and why?

Under the sea

- ★ Which texture are you most drawn to and why?
- ★ Choose a texture – how does this texture feel?
- ★ Choose a texture – what is this texture similar to?

BLOCK 5:4

Theme: MESSAGES

Strand: MANAGE

The Messages theme is the vehicle to the Manage Jellyfish strand. Manage helps us to acknowledge thoughts, feelings and situations safely. Messages are a means of passing on information. How our emotions react to the messages given and received depends upon the nature and content of the message. Through the Messages theme we can give ourselves the positive information we need and learn not to accept the negative messages from ourselves and others.

Initial gathering: brushing off/Jellyfish breathing/Jellyfish wave

Exploring the theme: choose from...

Task	**Bodywork**
Discuss the types of messages that can be sent and received; highlight that messages can make people feel different emotions, e.g. loved, upset, special, happy or angry. Prior to the class cut and roll the **coded messages** and insert them into empty bottles or jars. Ask the children to choose a container they are drawn to and using the **special writing characters** (and **decoded messages**), decode the message. Each message gifts the child a positive statement for them to keep.	★ Envelope ★ Phone call ★ Bottle ★ Email ★ Direct
Massage	**Visualization**
★ **Permission, hug and frame** ★ Write a message ★ Type a message ★ Text a message ★ Draw a message ★ Send a message ★ **Personal signature and hug**	**See Messages visualization**

Creative expression: to support children to manage their thoughts and feelings through messages, you may like to:

★ Provide the **postcard template**

★ Invite children to use a voice recorder to create their own messages

★ Allow free choice

Final gathering: Jellyfish gallery

Questions to support creative chatter:

On the shore

★ Has this message been given or received?

★ Who could this message be for?

★ What is this message about?

Under the sea

★ How would it feel to give this message to someone?

★ How would it feel to receive this message from someone?

★ Is this a message you would like to keep or throw away?

BLOCK 5:5

Theme: **BUTTERFLIES**   Strand: **DEVELOP**

The Butterflies theme is the vehicle to the Develop Jellyfish strand. Develop helps us to grow as individuals, in our relationships and in our lives. It helps us to explore possibilities and move forwards and make changes for the better. Within the Butterfly theme, who or what the caterpillar was previously is immaterial, as the butterfly who emerges anew is who it truly wishes to be.

Initial gathering: brushing off/Jellyfish breathing/Jellyfish wave

Exploring the theme: choose from...

Task	Bodywork
Give each child a circle of coloured paper. Discuss and share suggestions for uncomfortable/negative feelings and behaviours. Ask the children to write/draw one of these on their circle. Build a caterpillar body using the circles and **caterpillar head**. Explain to the group that the caterpillar has been all of these things but is now ready to shed them. Gather all the circles up and place them in a box (chrysalis). Shake the box and take out a butterfly (toy, model or picture) to symbolize this new beginning.	★ Egg ★ Caterpillar ★ Chrysalis ★ Emerge ★ Butterfly
Massage	**Visualization**
★ **Permission, hug and frame** ★ The body ★ Wing shape ★ Wing pattern ★ Antennae ★ Flutter and fly ★ **Personal signature and hug**	**See Butterflies visualization**

Creative expression: to support children to develop who they would like to be, you may like to:

- ★ Provide the **butterfly template**
- ★ Invite children to make a symmetrical butterfly, painting one half then folding over the paper
- ★ Allow free choice

Final gathering: Jellyfish gallery

Questions to support creative chatter:

On the shore

- ★ What is your favourite thing about this butterfly?
- ★ Where might someone find a butterfly like this?
- ★ How would it feel to be able to fly like this butterfly?

Under the sea

- ★ What sort of caterpillar did this butterfly used to be?
- ★ How does this butterfly feel to finally be a butterfly?
- ★ What will this butterfly be able to do?

BLOCK 5: RESOURCES

Theme	Task	Bodywork	Massage	Visualization	Creative expression
Books	Wrapped book	Books	As listed on class plans	Books	Book cover template
Hot Air Balloons	Balloons Marker pens Cups	Hot Air Balloons		Hot Air Balloons	Hot air balloon template
Textures	Feely bag containing a range of different textures	Textures		Textures	Patchwork template Wax crayons Foil embossing sheets Dough
Messages	Coded messages Special writing characters (B2:2) Decoded messages Empty jars and bottles	Messages		Messages	Postcard template Voice recorder
Butterflies	Caterpillar head Coloured paper circles Box Model or image of butterfly	Butterflies		Butterflies	Butterfly template

Highlighted items are provided in this book: resources are at the end of this block, massage suggestions are included in the class plans and bodywork illustrations and visualization outlines are listed at the end of the book.

BOOKS B5:1 BOOK COVER TEMPLATE

HOT AIR BALLOONS B5:2 HOT AIR BALLOON TEMPLATE

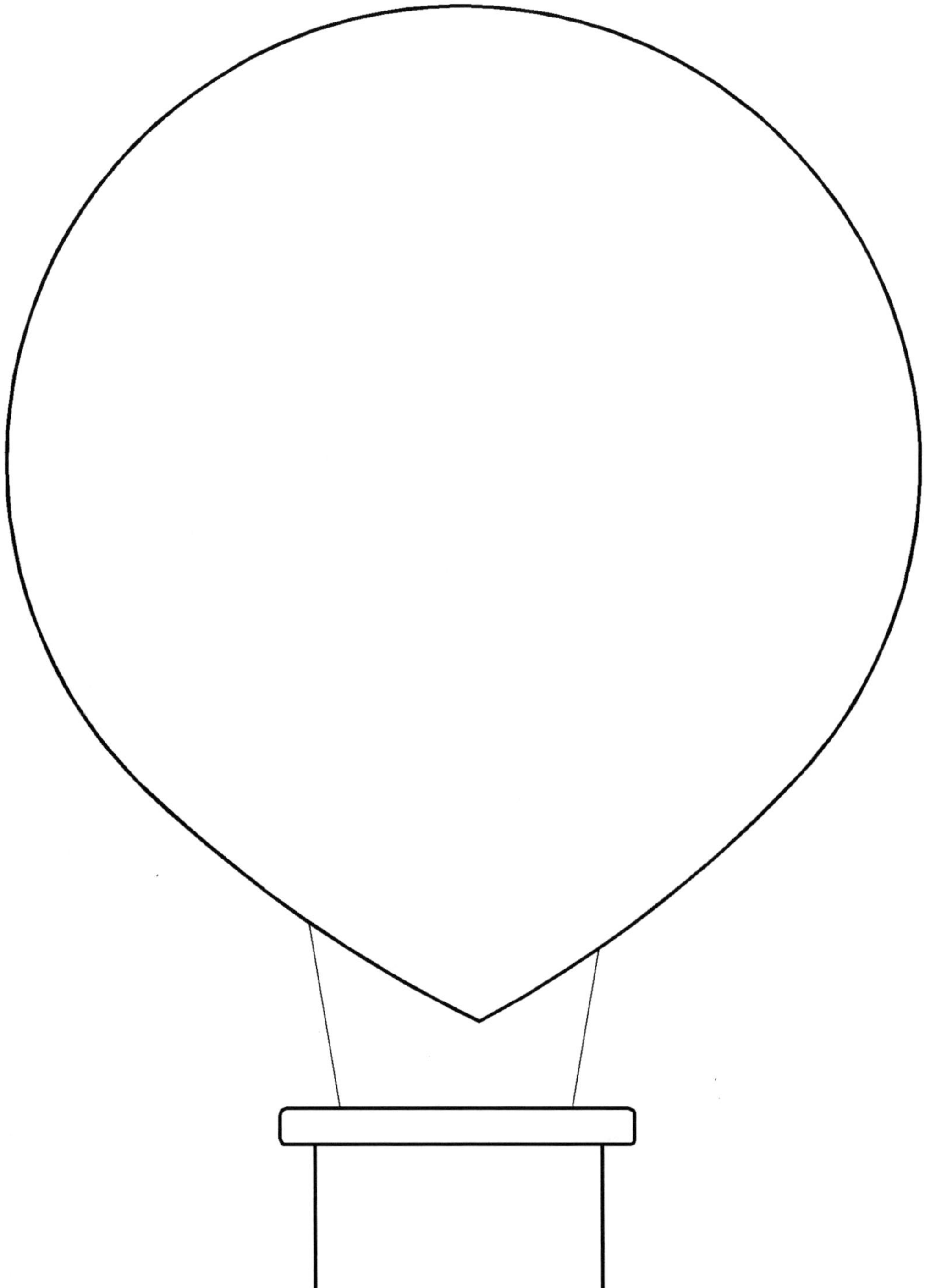

TEXTURES B5:3 PATCHWORK TEMPLATE

MESSAGES B5:4 CODED MESSAGES

(To be used in conjunction with the special writing characters B2:2)

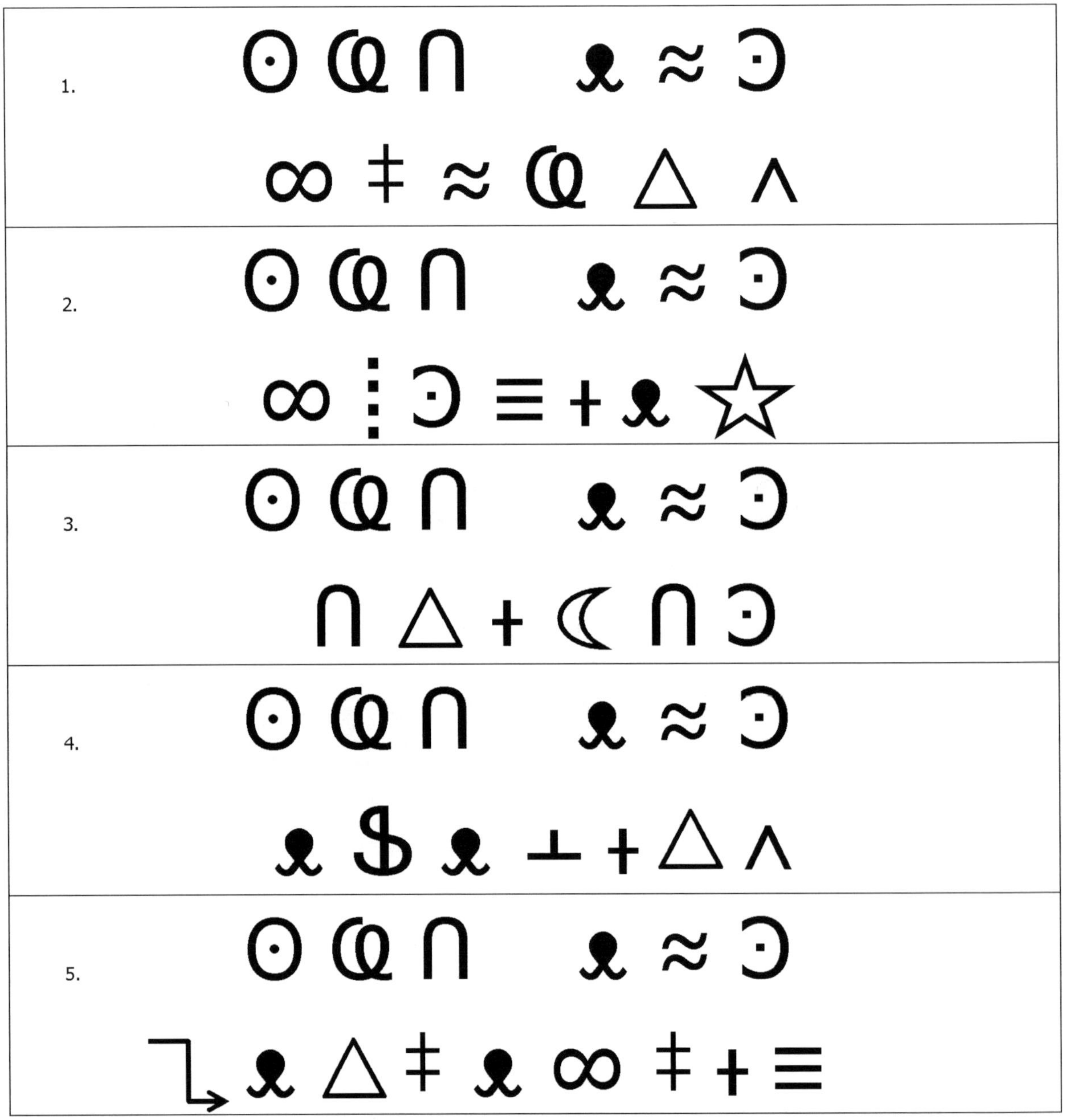

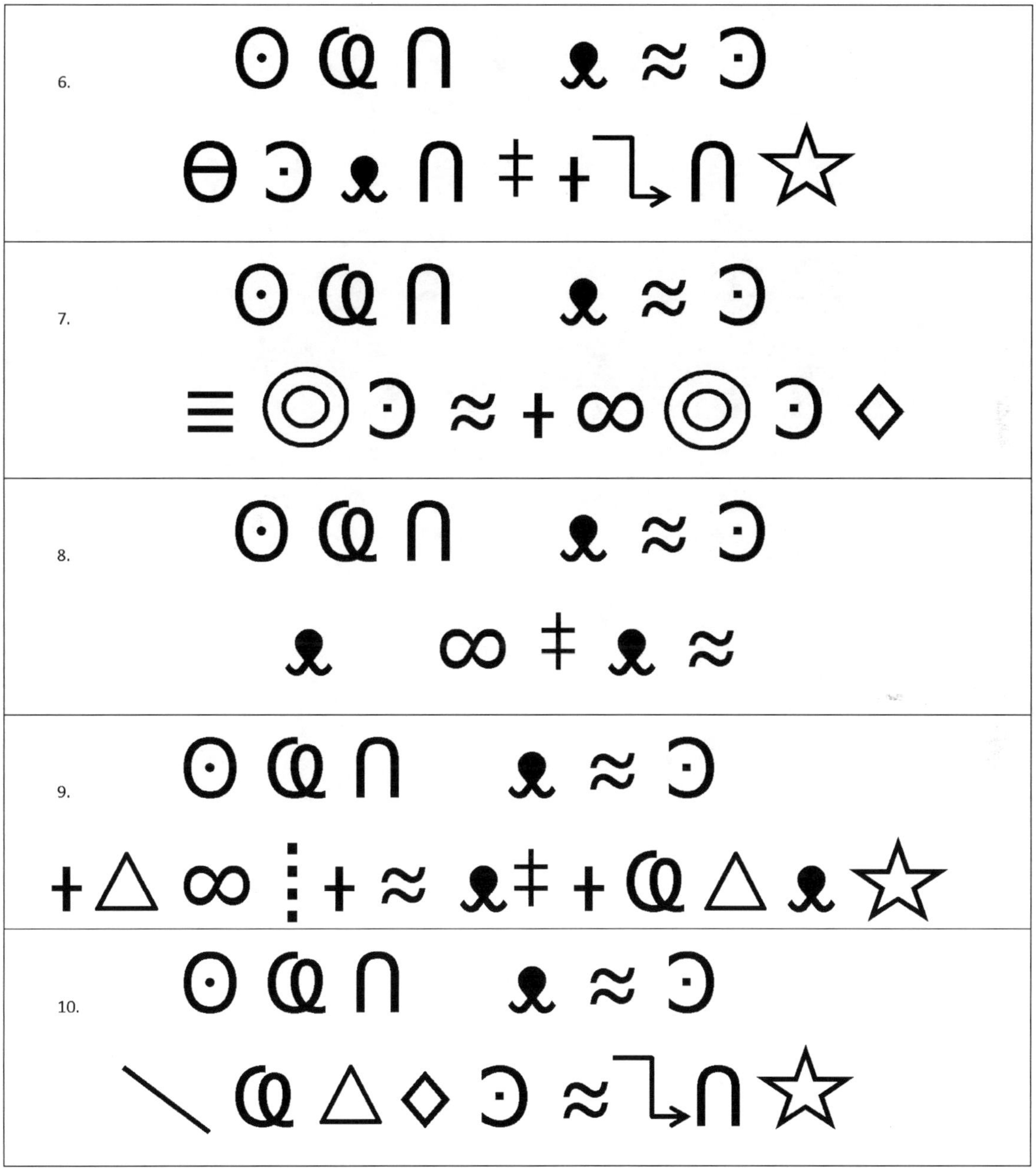
6.
7.
8.
9.
10.

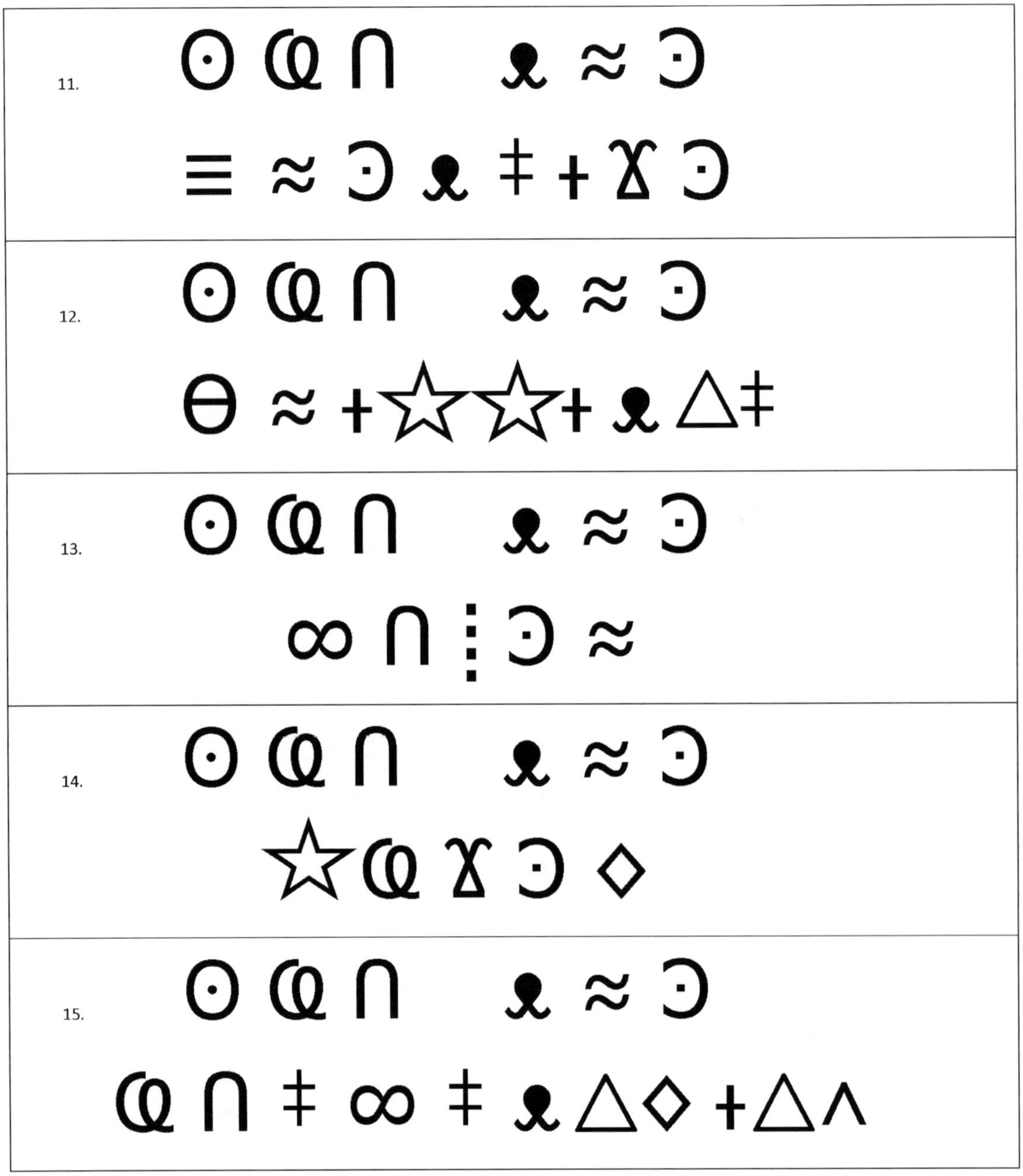
11.
12.
13.
14.
15.

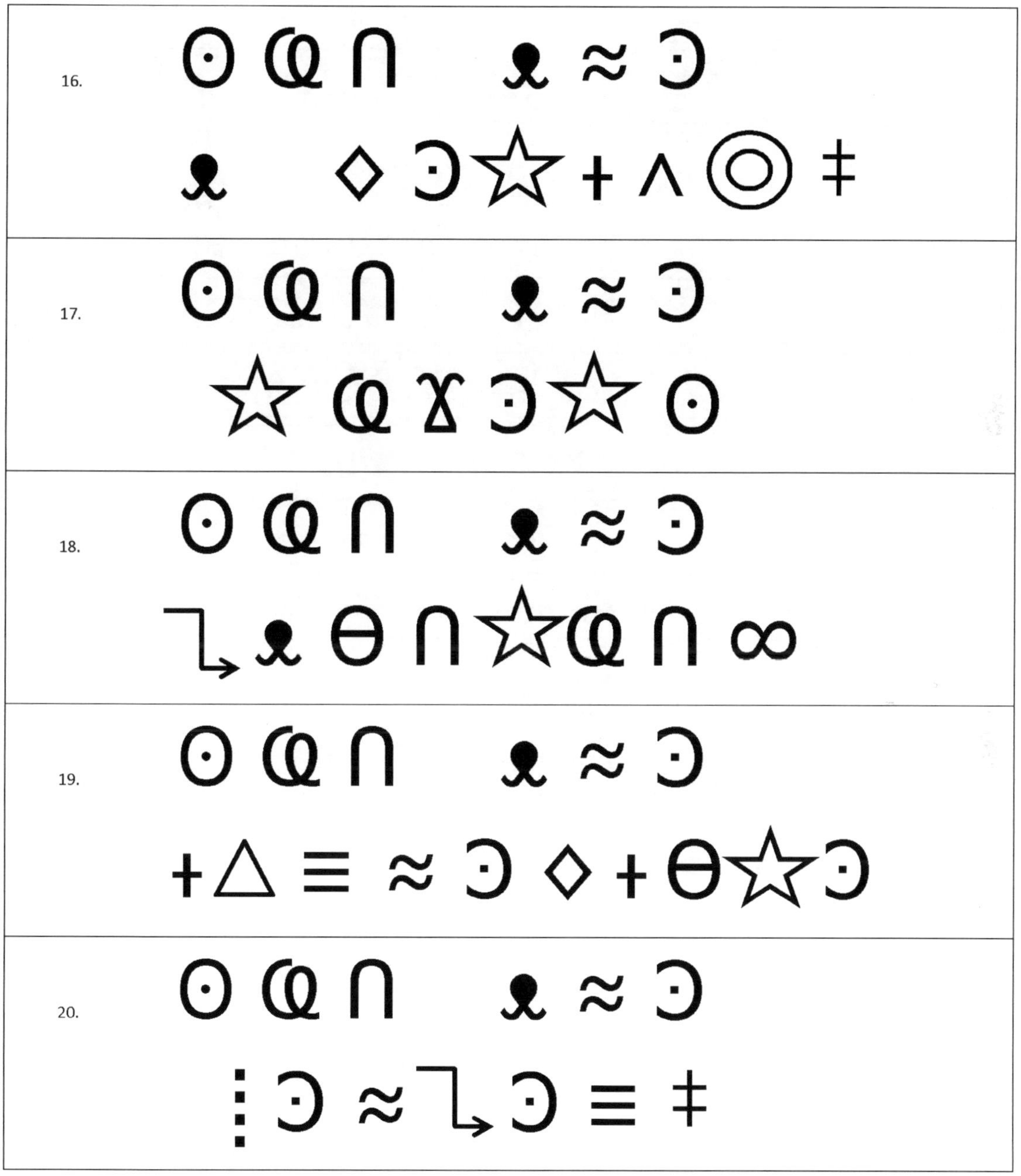
16.
17.
18.
19.
20.

MESSAGES B5:4 DECODED MESSAGES

1.	You are strong
2.	You are special
3.	You are unique
4.	You are amazing
5.	You are fantastic
6.	You are beautiful
7.	You are cherished
8.	You are a star
9.	You are inspirational
10.	You are wonderful
11.	You are creative
12.	You are brilliant
13.	You are super
14.	You are loved
15.	You are outstanding
16.	You are a delight
17.	You are lovely
18.	You are fabulous
19.	You are incredible
20.	You are perfect

MESSAGES B5:4 POSTCARD TEMPLATE

BUTTERFLIES B5:5 CATERPILLAR HEAD

BUTTERFLIES B5:5 BUTTERFLY TEMPLATE

Block 6

CLASS PLANS AND RESOURCES

BLOCK 6:1

Theme: **ROCKS**

Strand: **DISCOVER**

The Rocks theme is the vehicle for the Discover Jellyfish strand and so enables us to safely discover how we see ourselves, relationships with others and the world around us. Rocks have an air of strength, beauty and consistency but can also be seen as hard, cold and distant. Through rocks we can discover more of how we view ourselves and harness the qualities we share with rocks in a positive way.

Initial gathering: brushing off/Jellyfish breathing/Jellyfish wave

Exploring the theme: choose from…

Task	**Bodywork**
Display a small collection of rocks on the focus point. Hand the rocks around the circle and ask the group for words to describe them. Make a list of the suggestions on a large sheet of paper or flip chart. Once you feel enough words have been collected, ask the children to place the rocks back on the focal point. Now recap on the words by reading them aloud and ask the children what they notice about the list. Conclude that some rocks have similar qualities but each one is also unique and has its own special qualities. No rock is better than any of the other; they are all just different and that is ok.	★ Strong, silent rock This single pose is intended to be used for the duration of the bodywork. Encourage children to remain as still as possible, focusing on deep breathing, regular breaths and imagining themselves as a strong, silent rock.
Massage	**Visualization**
★ **Permission, hug and frame** ★ Dig the earth ★ A round smooth rock ★ A sharp, jagged rock ★ A cluster of small crystals ★ A large, layered rock ★ **Personal signature and hug**	**See Rocks visualization**

Creative expression: to support children to discover some of their own unique qualities, you may like to:

- ★ Provide the **cave template** on which children can draw their rock
- ★ Invite the children to create their own rock using clay
- ★ Allow free choice

Final gathering: Jellyfish gallery

Questions to support creative chatter:

On the shore

- ★ Where is this cave?
- ★ What sort of rock is in this cave?
- ★ Who knows this rock is in there?

Under the sea

- ★ How would you describe this rock?
- ★ What does this rock like/dislike about itself?
- ★ If you could choose one of this rock's qualities, what would it be?

BLOCK 6:2

Theme: **JELLYFISH FLURRY**

Strand: **EXPLORE**

The Jellyfish Flurry theme is the vehicle to the Explore Jellyfish strand. Through Explore we seek to find out more about what we have discovered and hope to gain a greater understanding and appreciation of who we are. At Be the Jellyfish we use 'flurry' as the collective noun for jellyfish. Creating and exploring a group of jellyfish is a safe way to explore how we view ourselves amongst a group and how we interact with others.

Initial gathering: brushing off/Jellyfish breathing/Jellyfish wave

Exploring the theme: choose from...

Task	**Bodywork**
Using any five of the **Jellyfish picture cards** (B1:1), explain to the group that you will be picking a card at random and you would like them to act out that jellyfish. Once all of the jellyfish have been acted out, for each card, ask the children the following questions: ★ How did it feel to be this jellyfish? ★ What do people think/feel about this jellyfish? ★ What would you like to say to this jellyfish?	★ Quiet jellyfish ★ Lonely jellyfish ★ Friendly jellyfish ★ Confident jellyfish ★ Frightened jellyfish For this bodywork, children are to create the pose that they feel best represents each of the jellyfish.
Massage	**Visualization**
★ **Permission, hug and frame** ★ Deep down under the waves ★ A jellyfish is alone ★ Large jellyfish appears ★ Little jellyfish appears ★ All jellyfish bobbing and swimming together ★ **Personal signature and hug**	**See Jellyfish Flurry visualization**

Creative expression: to explore different emotions, you may like to:

- Provide the **flurry template**
- Invite the children to create their own under-the-sea jellyfish scene
- Allow free choice

Final gathering: Jellyfish gallery

Questions to support creative chatter:

On the shore

- Where are these jellyfish?
- How are each of these jellyfish feeling today?
- If these jellyfish could speak, what would they be saying?

Under the sea

- Choose a jellyfish. Can you tell me three things about that jellyfish?
- Choose any two jellyfish. What would they say to one another?
- If you could move any of the jellyfish around, where would you place them and why?

BLOCK 6:3

Theme: **PUPPETS**

Strand: **EXPRESS**

The Puppets theme is the vehicle to the Express Jellyfish strand. Express invites us to explore the possibilities of our imagination, our thoughts and our feelings. As puppet master we can make the puppet feel, behave, act and be whoever we want it to be. There is no right or wrong; the puppet is who we choose it to be.

Initial gathering: brushing off/Jellyfish breathing/Jellyfish wave

Exploring the theme: choose from…

Task	**Bodywork**
Provide a collection of different puppets. Invite the children to choose one. One at a time the puppet should introduce themselves to the puppet sitting on their left-hand side. Encourage the children to give their puppet the voice/persona they wish. Continue around the circle until all the puppets have been introduced.	★ Seated puppet ★ Loose strings ★ Tight strings ★ Arm-leg lift ★ Head turn
Massage	**Visualization**
★ **Permission, hug and frame** ★ Body of puppet ★ Arms and legs ★ A face ★ An emotion ★ Strings ★ **Personal signature and hug**	**See Puppets visualization**

Creative expression: to support children to express themselves through puppets, you may like to:

- ★ Provide the **puppet template**
- ★ Invite the children to make their own wooden spoon puppet
- ★ Allow free choice

Final gathering: Jellyfish gallery

Questions to support creative chatter:

On the shore

- ★ What kind of puppet is this?
- ★ Who does this puppet belong to?
- ★ Where is this puppet kept?

Under the sea

- ★ How might this puppet feel when it is not being used?
- ★ How might this puppet feel when it is being used?
- ★ What sound does this puppet make?

BLOCK 6:4

Theme: **ANGELS**

Strand: **MANAGE**

The Angels theme is the vehicle to the Manage Jellyfish strand. Manage helps us to acknowledge thoughts, feelings and situations safely. The protective nature associated with angels makes them a natural theme for the Manage strand. The idea of an angel who listens without judgement and watches over you is a powerful medium when looking for guidance and support.

Initial gathering: brushing off/Jellyfish breathing/Jellyfish wave

Exploring the theme: choose from...

Task	Bodywork
Discuss how angels make us feel better. Give each child an **angel 1 template**. Ask them to write one thing they wish the angel to protect or take away. Write on the line on the right-hand side. Form the angel into a cone and place the left-hand edge over the right-hand edge to conceal the writing. Staple the edges together. To finish their angels, children can add wings and a halo using pipe cleaners. Place the angels around the **focal point**.	★ Heavenly angel ★ Protective angel ★ Guardian angel ★ Rising angel ★ Halo
Massage	**Visualization**
★ **Permission, hug and frame** ★ Clouds ★ Streams of light ★ Angel wings ★ Halo circles ★ Prayers ★ **Personal signature and hug**	**See Angels visualization**

Creative expression: to support children to manage some of the more challenging aspects of their lives, you may like to:

- ★ Provide the **angel 2 template**
- ★ Invite children to create their own angel
- ★ Allow free choice

Final gathering: Jellyfish gallery

Questions to support creative chatter:

On the shore

- ★ Where is this angel from?
- ★ What is special about this angel?
- ★ What sort of things could this angel look after?

Under the sea

- ★ How might it feel to have this angel looking out for you?
- ★ What sort of things could this angel do?
- ★ If this angel could speak, what would it say?

BLOCK 6:5

Theme: **INVENTIONS** Strand: **DEVELOP**

The Inventions theme is the vehicle to the Develop Jellyfish strand. Develop helps us to grow as individuals, in our relationships and in our lives. It helps us to explore possibilities, move forward and make changes for the better. Inventions invites us to become inventors. As inventors we design what we need for ourselves in order to live the life we would like.

Initial gathering: brushing off/Jellyfish breathing/Jellyfish wave

Exploring the theme: choose from...

Task	Bodywork
Explain to the children that they are going to create a tool kit; one that they can use on a daily basis. The kit will contain all the things (tools) that they need to feel good. Discuss possibilities. Using the **my tool kit template** invite children to write or draw the tool or tools they need before folding along the dotted lines to secure the tool kit. Remind the group that this can be taken out and used whenever required and additional tools may be added at any time.	★ Question ★ Thinking ★ Light bulb (idea) ★ Workbench ★ Machine
Massage	**Visualization**
★ **Permission, hug and frame** ★ Ideas go in ★ Press the buttons ★ Flashing lights ★ Turning dials ★ Invention comes out ★ **Personal signature and hug**	**See Inventions visualization**

Creative expression: to support children to develop the qualities that they feel they need, you may like to:

★ Provide the **workbench template**

★ Invite children to create their own invention using junk items such as cardboard boxes, yogurt pots, bottle tops and drinking straws

★ Allow free choice

Final gathering: Jellyfish gallery

Questions to support creative chatter:

On the shore

★ What does this invention do?

★ Why is this invention useful?

★ Where could someone get an invention like this?

Under the sea

★ When could an invention like this be used?

★ Who would benefit from having an invention like this?

★ If you had this invention, what would you do with it?

BLOCK 6: RESOURCES

Theme	Task	Bodywork	Massage	Visualization	Creative expression
Rocks	Small collection of different rocks	Rocks	As listed on class plans	Rocks	Cave template Clay
Jellyfish Flurry	Jellyfish picture cards (B1:1)	Jellyfish Flurry		Jellyfish Flurry	Flurry template
Puppets	A variety of puppets	Puppets		Puppets	Puppet template Wooden spoons Fabric
Angels	Angel 1 template Stapler Pipe cleaners	Angels		Angels	Angel 2 template
Inventions	My tool kit template	Inventions		Inventions	Workbench template Junk items, e.g. cardboard boxes, yogurt pots, bottle tops, drinking straws

Highlighted items are provided in this book: resources are at the end of this block, massage suggestions are included in the class plans, and bodywork illustrations and visualization outlines are listed at the end of the book.

ROCKS B6:1 CAVE TEMPLATE

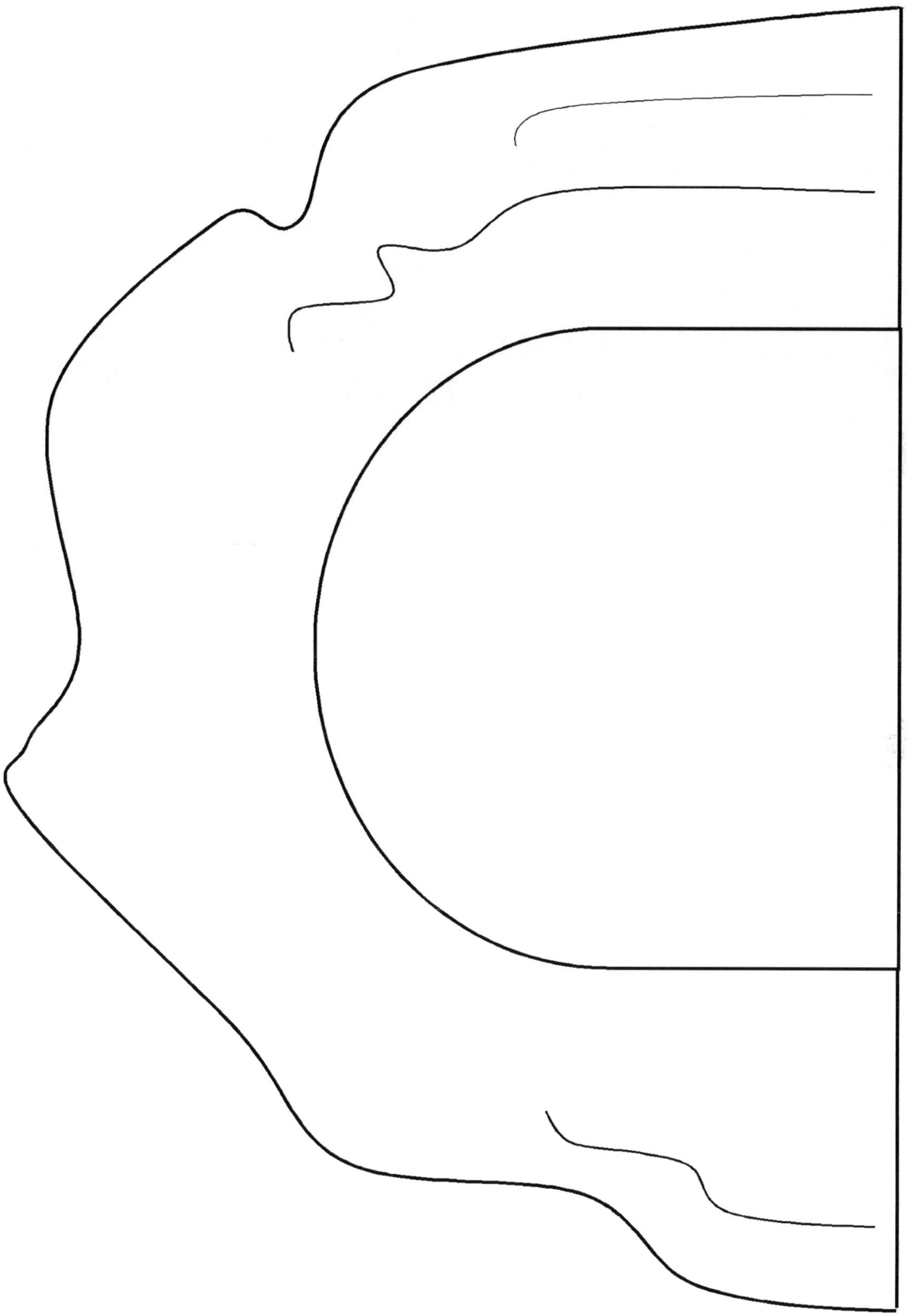

JELLYFISH FLURRY B6:2 FLURRY TEMPLATE

PUPPETS B6:3 PUPPET TEMPLATE

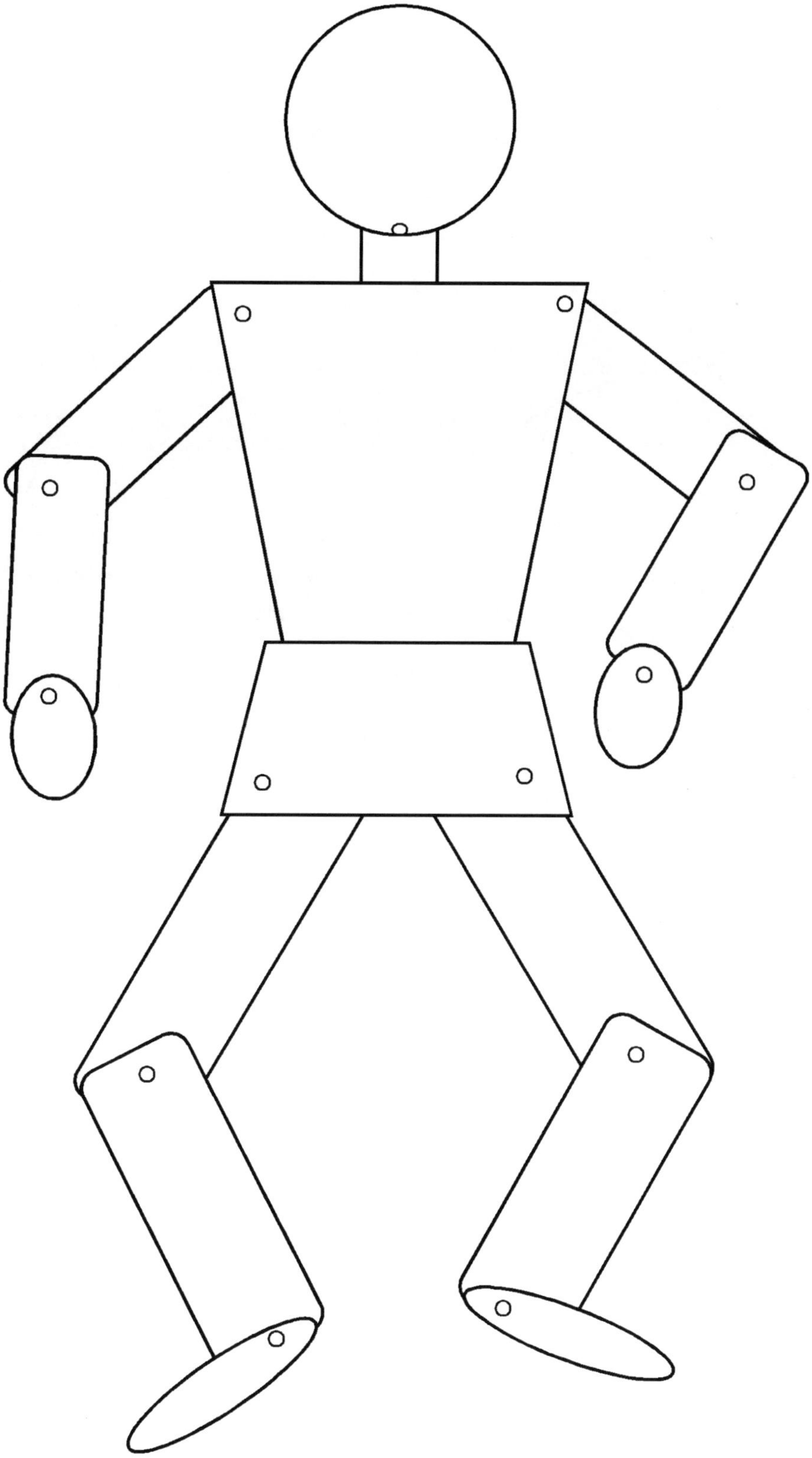

ANGELS B6:4 ANGEL 1 TEMPLATE

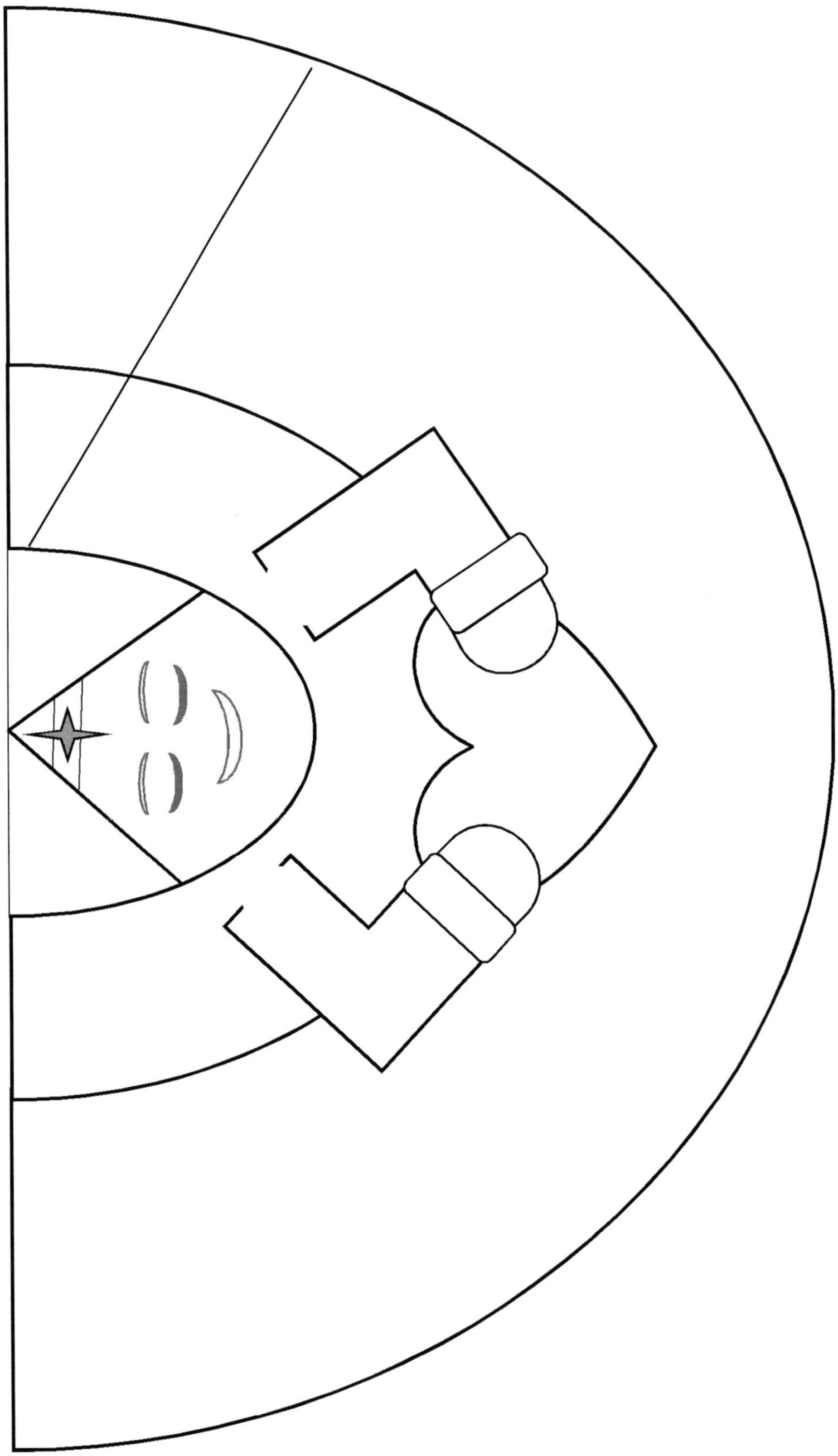

ANGELS B6:4 ANGEL 2 TEMPLATE

INVENTORS B6:5 MY TOOL KIT TEMPLATE

MY TOOL KIT

INVENTORS B6:5 WORKBENCH TEMPLATE

TASKS

About tasks

Tasks combine a number of learning styles for **exploring the theme** and are closely linked to **Jellyfish strands**. Feel confident using your own teaching style to deliver and adapt the task to suit the child or children who you are working with. Most tasks are undertaken in the **gathering place** and, unless they say otherwise, require the children to sit in a circle.

Enabling tasks

If a task is chosen for **exploring the theme**, it is essential that the activity is prepared beforehand. Be the Jellyfish provide many of the resources necessary for the tasks; however, some will need to be acquired by the Jellyfish teacher. Time invested in preparing resources for a task is important to ensure the best possible experience and intended outcome.

BODYWORK

About bodywork

Bodywork comprises a series of poses, stretches and movements used to help children feel calm, strong and ready to create. It is also considered an accessible, whole-body approach in which to **explore the theme**.

Enabling bodywork

Generally, there are five bodywork aspects per themed class. Each set should be repeated at least three times and held for at least three deep breaths.

Where poses and stretches are focused on one side of the body, unless already depicted in a sequence, it is necessary to repeat them on the opposite side in order to retain the body's natural balance.

Model slow, careful, fluid movements. Bodywork should not be rushed and children may need to be taught to slow down in order to maintain the atmosphere of the room and avoid injury.

Always ensure that there is sufficient space to participate and that the area has been cleared of hazards.

To warm up, a gentle stretch and body wiggle is ideal. Name and show the children each pose before they attempt them. Explain that bodywork is not about perfection and exact replication, just effort. Refer to the **Jellyfish motto.** The most important thing is to model focus, concentration and regular, deep breathing. If necessary, exaggerate the breaths until the children are familiar with how to breathe during bodywork.

Praise good practice, especially with children who find bodywork challenging.

JELLYFISH B1:1

Jellyfish bell

Bobbing jellyfish

Darting jellyfish

Wibbly wobbly jellyfish

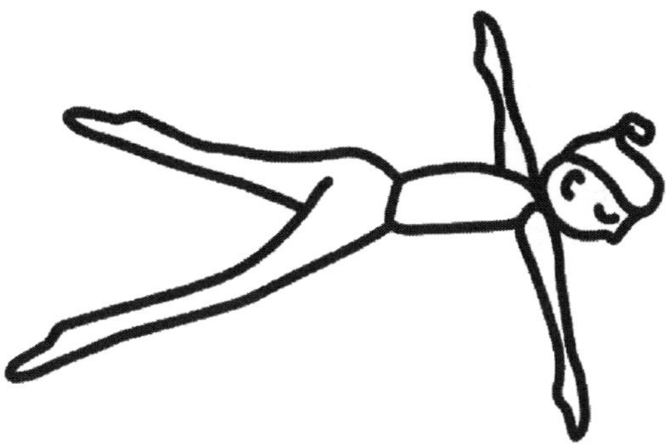

Resting jellyfish

ELEMENTS B1:2

Fire one

Fire two

Wind

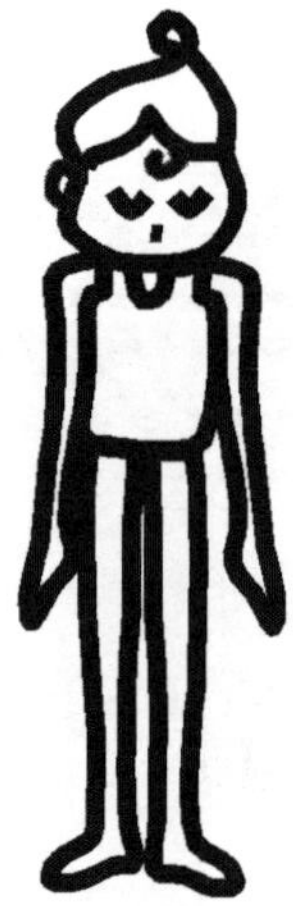

Earth

Water

MUSIC B1:3

Ear

Sound wave

Treble clef

Crotchet

Line of music

TREASURE B1:4

Receive

Cherish

Contain

Hide

Reveal

FANTASY B1:5

Giant

Witch's hat

Fairy

Unicorn

Pegasus

COLOUR B2:1

Squat down

Scoop up a colour

Colour to heart

Colour to head

Rain colour down

SPECIAL PLACES B2:2

Safe

Rested

Secure

Peaceful

Be yourself

DREAMS B2:3

Fly

Climb

Invisible

Royal

Mermaid

MAGIC B2:4

Magic star

Magic broom

Magic potion

Magic wand

Magic book

CHARACTERS B2:5

Confident

In love

Shy

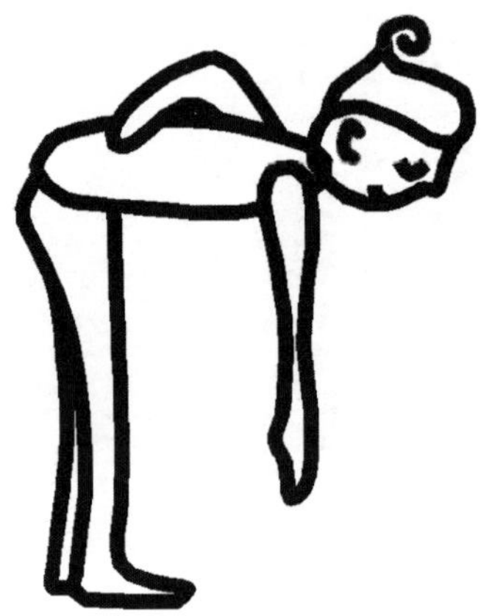

Old

Angry

ANIMALS B3:1

Tiger

Mouse

Swan

Frog

Giraffe

DEEP SPACE B3:2

Sun star

Planet

Shooting star

Big Dipper

Orion's Belt

WEATHER B3:3

Raindrop

Lightning

Sun

Snowflake

Tornado

SECRET GARDEN B3:4

Seed

Grow one

Grow two

Grow three

Bloom

MIRRORS AND MASKS B3:5

Mirror one

Mirror two

Mirror three

Mirror four

Mask

CIRCUS B4:1

Ringmaster

Strongman

Tightrope walker

Juggler

Unicyclist

DESERTS B4:2

Dune

Cactus

Meerkat

Camel

Snake

HATS AND HEADDRESSES B4:3

Top hat

Feather headdress

Bonnet

Turban

Crown

POCKETS B4:4

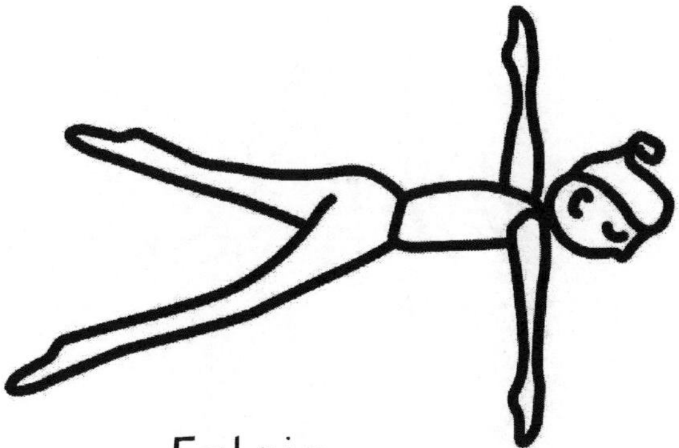

Fabric

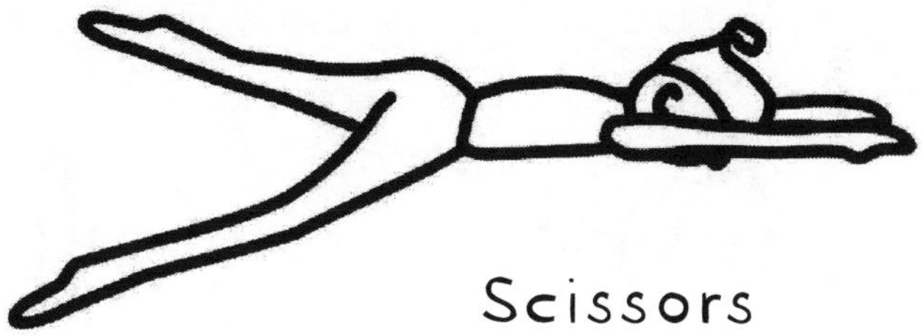

Scissors

Needle

Stitch

Pocket

FOOTPRINTS B4:5

BOOKS B5:1

Closed book

Open book

Reader 1

Reader 2

Reader 3

HOT AIR BALLOONS B5:2

Basket

Strings

Balloon

Take off

Fly away

TEXTURES B5:3

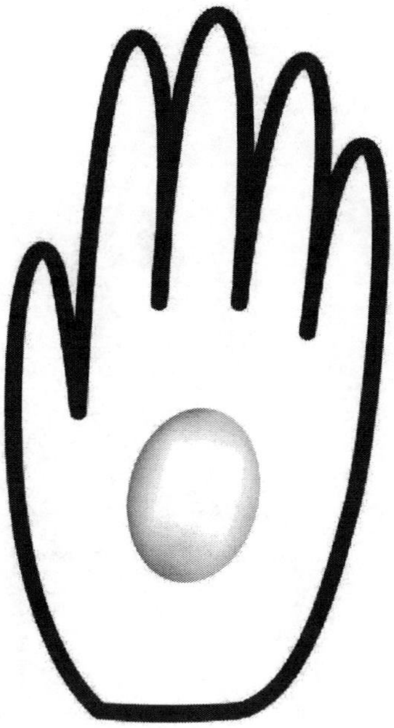

Smooth touch

Spiky touch

Bumpy touch

Rough touch

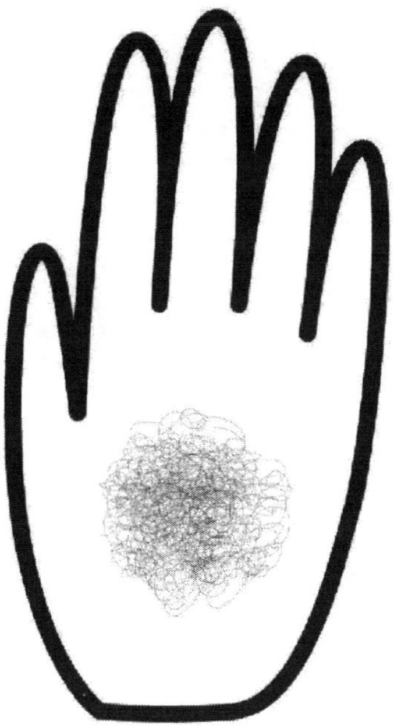

Fluffy touch

MESSAGES B5:4

Envelope

Phone call

Bottle

Email

Direct

BUTTERFLIES B5:5

Egg

Caterpillar

Chrysalis

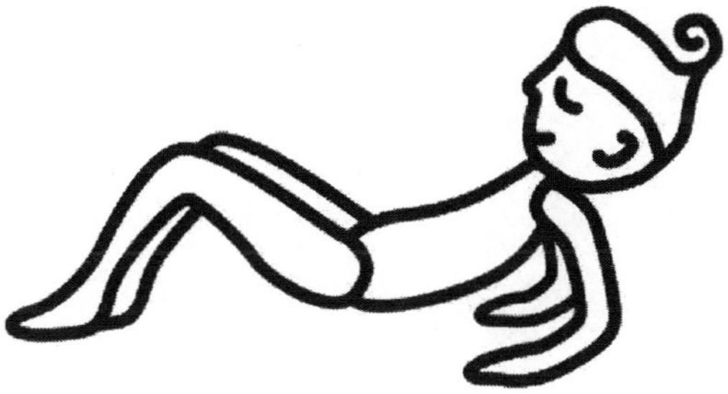

Emerge

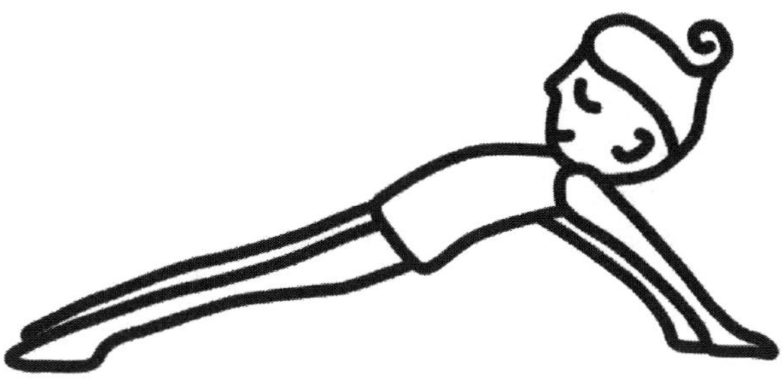

Butterfly

ROCKS B6:1

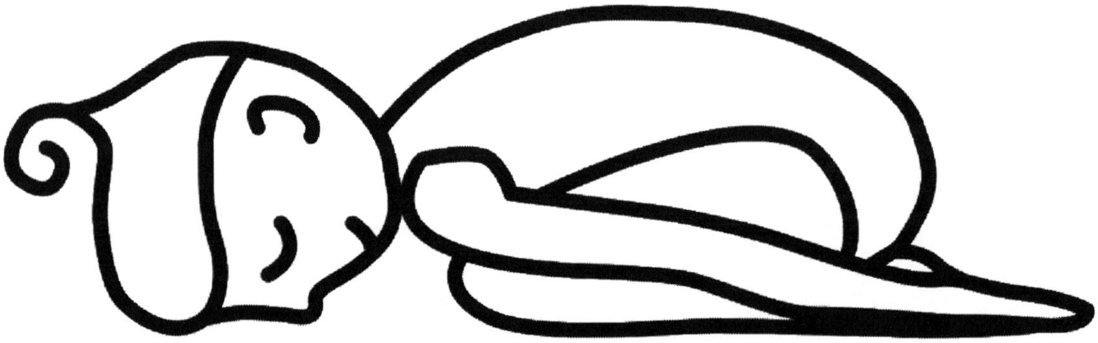

Strong, silent rock

JELLYFISH FLURRY B6:2

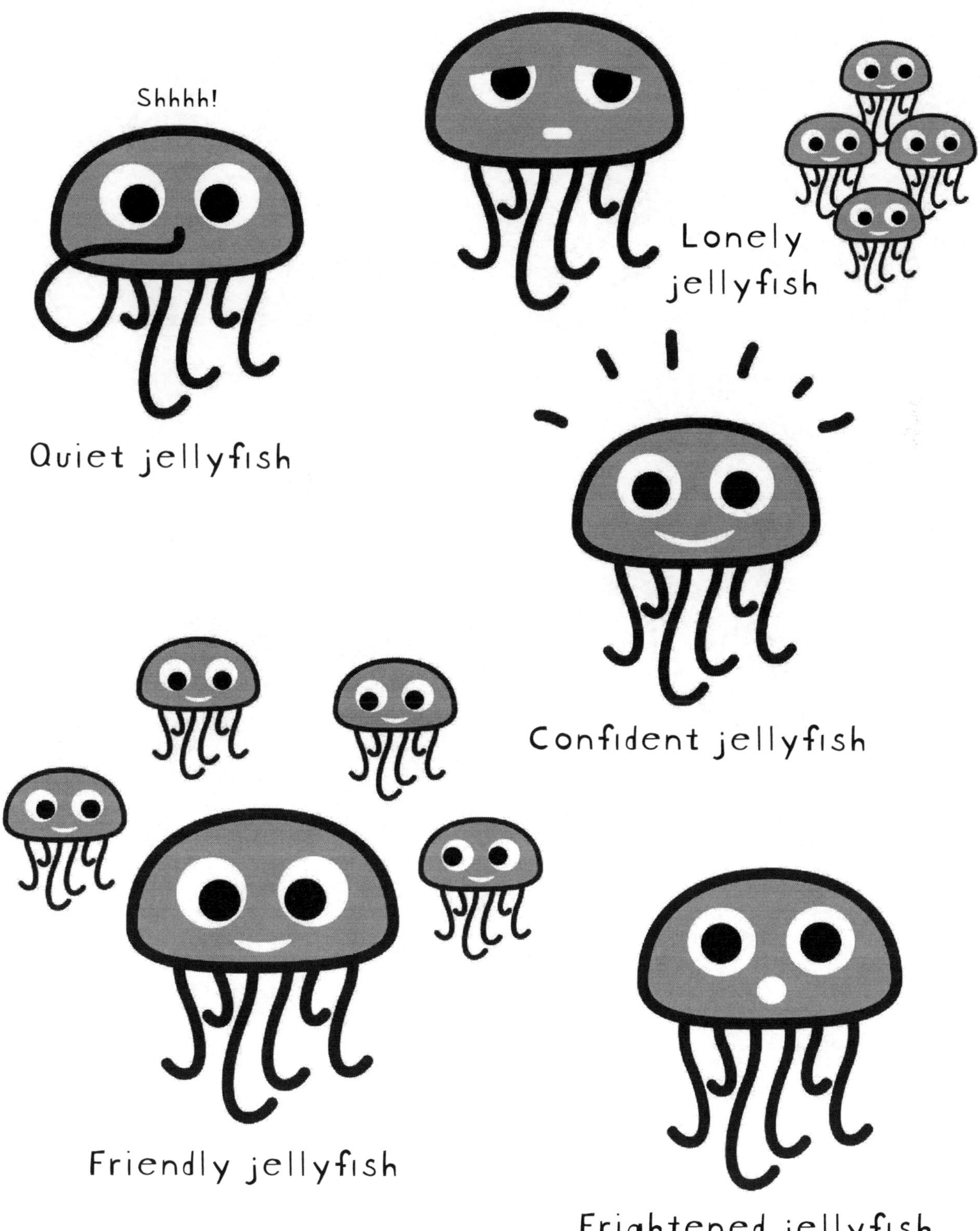

PUPPETS B6:3

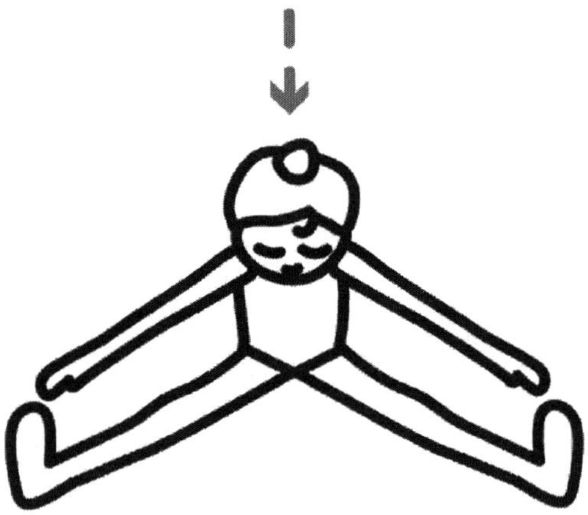

Seated puppet

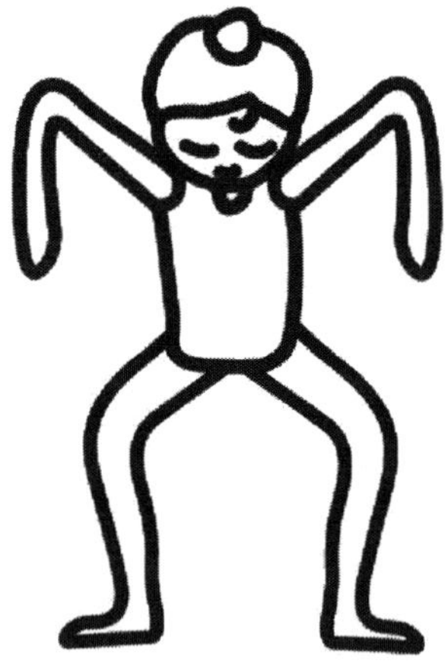

Loose strings

Tight strings

Arm-leg lift

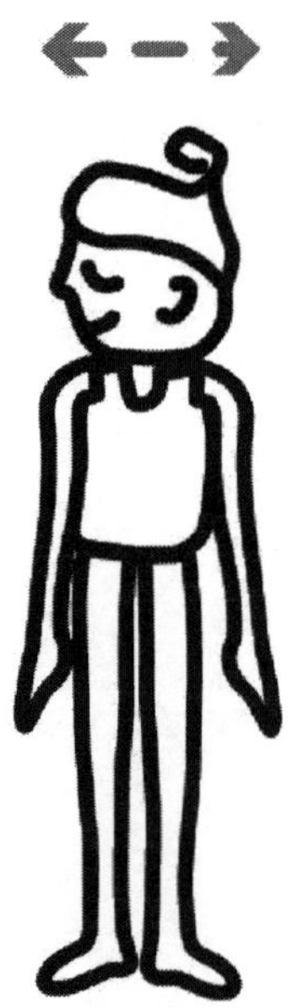

Head turn

ANGELS B6:4

Heavenly angel

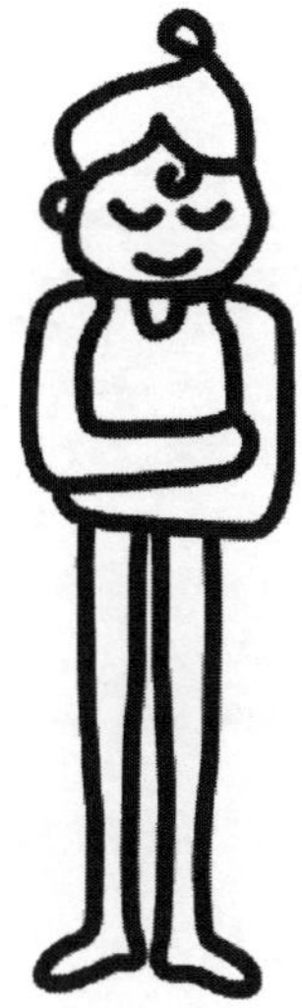

Protective angel

Guardian angel

Rising angel

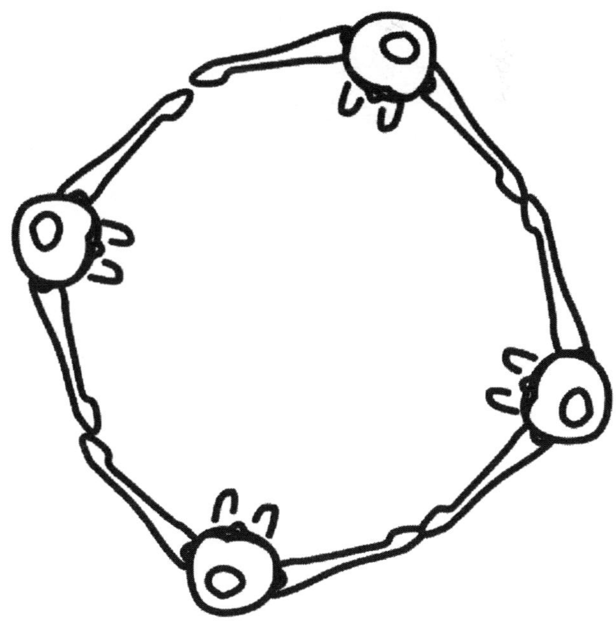

Halo

INVENTIONS B6:5

Question

Thinking

Light bulb (idea)

Workbench

Machine

MASSAGE

About massage

At Be the Jellyfish the word 'massage' is used to describe the action of drawing on the back of another person, using the fingers or the palm of the hand. This form of massage is not a set of learnt strokes but a form of expression and creativity. It is a response to keywords, suggestions and instructions.

Massage provides an opportunity to explore the theme in a tactile, non-committal way. Through massage children experience what it is like to give and receive positive touch. They are also encouraged to recognize and give voice to when touch is not positive or appropriate. It empowers children with choice and encourages positive body image and acceptance. The giving and receiving of massage is also a relaxation and mindfulness tool that creates a sense of calm and wellbeing.

Be the Jellyfish rules of massage

Jellyfish teachers are only permitted to instruct; they do not massage children or allow children to massage them.

Children should always:

- Ask the **permission** of the person they intend to massage
- Be gentle when massaging
- Say thank you to the person they have massaged

Enabling massage

When choosing a partner to massage with, children must make sure that their partner gives their consent to be massaged.

Teach children that they may use finger/s or the palm of their hand to massage. Encourage the group to experiment with the correct pressure for massage. This should not be too hard or too soft to avoid the action tickling or hurting their partner.

Every massage begins by lightly gripping both upper arms, then moving hands slowly up to the shoulders. Gently **hug** the shoulders with the hands to finish the movement.

Next, children draw a **frame** on their partner's back so that the person being massaged will know where to expect touch. This way, a safe boundary that the partner is comfortable with is agreed before the massage begins.

Remember Jellyfish massage is a tactile response to the prompts given by the Jellyfish teacher leading the massage; Jellyfish teachers should feel free to add more detail and give possibilities for drawing. Reassure children that each massage may feel and look different to another person's massage. Refer to the **Jellyfish motto.**

Each massage should be repeated until the next drawing instruction/keyword is given by the Jellyfish teacher.

Children should be taught to design their **personal signature**; this is how they will finish every massage before the end **hug**. The **personal signature** may be a shape, initials or something completely different but important to them.

The massage ends by doing the reverse of the starting action. Place hands on shoulders and glide hands down to upper arms, finishing with a gentle **hug**.

MASSAGE SEQUENCE

Ask for permission

↓

Shoulder hug

↓

Draw frame

↓

Massage

↓

Personal signature

↓

Upper arm hug

↓

Thank you

Participation

Some children will not feel comfortable giving or receiving massage, so children should always be given the option of not participating. The reasons why they do not wish to give or receive massage should not be questioned.

Whether or not they are directly engaged in massage, all children will benefit from the calm created in the room. Below are some alternative options for any child who does not wish to participate:

- Massage on a cuddly toy
- Massage on the palm of your hand
- Massage on a surface such as a floor, cushion or table top
- Massage in a tray or table prepared with shaving foam
- Massage in sand
- Massage in water
- Massage using a massage tool
- Massage using a feather
- Massage wearing a glove

VISUALIZATION

About visualization

Visualization is intended as an auditory means for **exploring the theme**. It also helps to develop imagination, focus the mind and relax the body.

Enabling visualization

When children are preparing to listen to a visualization, it is important that the atmosphere is calm and peaceful and that there is no communication between them. Allow a few minutes for the children to settle into their own individual space, during which time music should be playing quietly in the background.

Visualization should begin and end in the same way so that the children recognize and become familiar with the start and finish of the activity.

To begin, the Jellyfish teacher must repeat these instructions:

- **Position** yourself comfortably
- **Listen** to my voice
- **Close** your eyes
- **Breathe** deeply – in through your nose and out through your mouth
- **Imagine** the story that you are about to hear in your mind

Note: As the children breathe, ask them to notice how their breath feels. To encourage a state of relaxation, invite the children to let go of any troubles or worries they may have. Teach the class to continue to breathe in and out gently and calmly, letting go of any thoughts.

To conclude, the Jellyfish teacher must repeat these instructions:

- **Time to wake** your jellyfish
- **Wiggle** your fingers and toes
- **Stretch out** your arms and your legs
- **Open** your eyes
- **Sit up** slowly

Jellyfish visualization B1:1

Picture yourself as a jellyfish, soft and free, floating on the top of the ocean. You are very safe and feeling relaxed. Bobbing on the surface of the water, you take in the blue sky. Notice how white and wispy the clouds are. Feel the warmth of the sun on your jellyfish skin; your body tingles with the sensation of the heat. You let the soft waves of the ocean lap against you; the water is inviting.

Take in what you look like. How big are you? What shape are you? What colour are you? Are you long and willowy or small and powerful? Or are you something completely different?

Allow yourself to sink slowly under the water. You feel warm and safe as you drift beneath the surface. Gently glide closer to the bottom. Notice that your body feels light and totally relaxed. You no longer feel your weight, only how wonderful it feels to keep dropping and gliding. The water is shimmering below you and the path is bright; the light is soft and calming. Breathe in and out slowly and sink further and further, deeper and deeper, lower and lower until you reach the bottom.

To your surprise, you see something glinting on the seabed. You are drawn towards it. Stretch out and reach for the hidden sparkle. As you do, feel something small and smooth in your tentacle. There, as clear as crystal, you see it! Notice the colour and how it dazzles; it is perfectly smooth, perfectly round and perfectly polished. Feel how heavy it is; are you surprised by its weight?

This special gift now belongs to you. It is filled with all the things that make you you, all the things that make you unique: your personality, your talents, your abilities and your potential. Maybe you recognize some of these already but there are still many to discover...

Now it is time to go. You look up to the surface and feel content. Begin to drift back slowly through the waters. You feel the warmth on your body as you approach the surface. Once there, feel the familiar feeling of bobbing on the water once again. You squeeze your tentacle tightly and remember you are holding your precious gift.

Elements visualization B1:2

Picture yourself looking at four different boxes. Each box has a lid so you cannot see what is inside. One of the boxes is blue, one is green, one is red and the final box is black. Notice which one you are attracted to first.

Go to the blue box. Gently remove the lid. You recognize the word *water* written on it. Peer into the box. What do you see in this space? Perhaps you see droplets, a wave, a whirlpool or something entirely different. Spend some time looking into this space. Is the water cool or warm? Is it calm or rough? Or is it something else? Do you see anything in the water? How does this box make you feel? Take a breath and place the lid back on the box.

Next move over to the green box. Gently remove the lid. You recognize the word *earth* written on it. Peer into the box. What do you see in this space? Perhaps you see rock, soil, sand or something entirely different. Spend some time looking into this space. Is the earth dry or wet? Is it hard or soft? Or is it something else? Do you see anything in the earth? How does this box make you feel? Take a breath and place the lid back on the box.

Now approach the red box. Gently remove the lid. You recognize the word *fire*. Peer into the box. What do you see in this space? Perhaps you see flames, a candle, a glowing light or something entirely different. Spend some time looking into this space. Is the fire warm or hot? Is it bright or faint? Or is it something else? Do you see anything in the fire? How does this box make you feel? Take a breath and place the lid back on the box.

Finally, take the black box. Gently remove the lid. You recognize the word *wind* written on it. Peer into the box. What do you see in this space? Perhaps you see a kite, trees blowing in the breeze, a tornado or something entirely different. Spend some time looking into this space. Is the wind cool or warm? Is it fierce or gentle? Or is it something else? Do you see anything in the wind? How does this box make you feel? Take a breath and place the lid back on the box.

Music visualization B1:3

Picture yourself standing in the centre of a multi-coloured, square-tiled floor. Look carefully at this special floor; each square is a different colour and when you walk across it, it will make a musical sound. Each of the tiles is marked with a symbol; no one square is the same.

Take in the colours around you and notice which, if any, of the symbols you are drawn to. Choose which ones you will step onto. This floor will help you to express how you're feeling. Each sound will be different; some are low and deep, others are soft and gentle and perhaps some are high, loud or bold. Many of the sounds have been created from musical instruments but some are sounds that are heard in everyday life.

Select which square you would like to begin with and make your way to that square. Press your foot confidently onto the tile and listen to the sound it makes. It may be very faint at first; perhaps you can barely hear it, or the loudness may surprise you. Keep stepping on the sound square and notice how it makes you feel. As you listen, try to recognize what kind of sound this is and what could have made it.

Continue on to the next square of your choosing. As you step forward, notice if this makes the same sound, a similar sound or something entirely different. How does it make you feel? Is it a feeling that you like?

You may want to step onto more squares, perhaps there is a clear path ahead that you would like to follow, or you may choose to stick to the sounds you have already heard. The choice is yours and the sounds that are made are personal to you. As you listen, notice if they remind you of anything. Do they create images in your mind or are they simply sounds? Remember there is no right or wrong. Some of them might not feel nice to experience and you can leave those squares if you wish.

For now, why not enjoy experimenting with all the different sounds this magical square tiled floor can create and the opportunity to express yourself using music.

Treasure visualization B1:4

Picture yourself relaxing alone on a beautiful sandy beach. Feel the sun beaming down on you and the soft sand under your feet. Run your fingers and toes through the warm sand as you breathe in the fresh sea air. Listen to the gentle lapping of the waves rolling onto the shore and feel the light breeze brush across your cheeks.

Look around at the pure, white sand stretching for miles, completely untouched, without a single footprint. Gaze at the turquoise sea; it is twinkling in the sunlight. The waves continue to curl over and crash against the beach. This is a wonderful place; you feel happy, calm and safe.

Notice that there is a golden spade lying next to you. I wonder what it is doing here. Glancing down, you realize that you are sitting on a spot that has been marked 'X'. Perhaps something is buried here? It is time to find out. With ease, you begin to dig in the sand. Feel the warmth of the sun on your back as you create a large hole. Soon, you hit something hard with the spade. What could it be? Use the palm of your hands to scoop the soft, crumbling sand away from the object. As the sand clears you realize you have discovered your own treasure chest!

Take in the chest. What does it look like? Is it large, medium sized or small? What is it decorated with? You want to look inside, so, with care, you open up the lid but find, to your surprise, that it is empty. It is now up to you to fill the treasure chest with whatever you want. It is a special place to keep your own items in. What would you like to put in your chest? You can always take things out again if you would like. Take a few moments to fill it up with things that are important to you. These could be objects, photos or even memories or people. It is entirely up to you.

When you are ready, seal the lid of your treasure chest and place it securely in the sand. It is time to rebury it. You can return to it another day if you would like to.

As you pat down the last pile of sand with your spade, you stare out at the calm, quiet ocean once more. Take in a deep breath. This really is a wonderful place to be.

Fantasy visualization B1:5

Picture yourself on the balcony of a castle. Place your hands securely on the rail. Look out at the view. What an amazing sight it is; it looks magnificent and so inviting. From high up here, what can you see? Perhaps you see lush, rolling hills and imposing, towering mountains, a vast ocean and a magical forest or a mysterious lake and a sweeping desert? Maybe there is a bustling town or a sleepy village? Or maybe you do not see anything at all. Just take a deep breath in and pause for a moment to appreciate whatever the view may be.

Now release your hands from the balcony rail and turn around. Step forward and find yourself in front of a large, ornate door, decorated in precious stones and glinting metals. Reach out and turn the twisted, snaking handle. The door opens easily. Step through it and into the castle. Take a moment to look at your surroundings. What do you see? It is exactly as you want it to be.

You feel safe here inside this strong, secure building and a smile appears on your face.

As you wander through the majestic rooms notice how this castle makes you feel. Take in what you see.

Does anything here seem familiar to you? You may like to invite someone you know to join you in your castle, or you may wish to remain by yourself. This is your castle so you can welcome whomever you like.

Within this castle you can be who you want to be. The castle belongs to you and mirrors who you truly are. You feel proud of your castle and smile a confident smile. It is time to choose if you would like to explore what is outside of your castle or if you would like to stay here. It is perfectly safe if you want to leave, but you don't have to. If you wish, take some time to enjoy wandering the paths outside the castle; maybe take a friend with you or simply choose to stay within its strong, secure walls. Remember, this is your castle and you can come and go as you wish.

Colours visualization B2:1

Picture a sky full of any and every colour you can imagine, all curling and swirling above you. It is a truly magical sight; like nothing you have ever seen. There is such a range of colours, from the brightest fluorescents to the softest hues. Some you can't even name. You see every shade and combination; the deepest and richest of tones to the palest, most subtle wisps of heavenly light.

For a moment, you turn your gaze from the vibrant, vivid sky and see laid out before you a blank canvas, a paintbrush and an empty palette. These are waiting to be used by you. How wonderful would it be to create a picture with the colours of the sky, filling the palette with any colour you would like?

Looking up, choose whichever colour your heart desires, reaching carefully to scoop it from the curling, swirling sky. It feels light and tingles in your palm. You gently cup the colour and then slide it into the first palette pocket. Notice it leaves no stain on your hand.

You need to fill your palette with five more colours. Take a few moments to stretch back up to the sky and choose them, one by one. These may be your favourite or ones you don't expect; perhaps you choose those that are very special to you.

When you are ready you can use your paintbrush to create a picture. This may be specific shapes, an image of something in particular or random combinations and patterns of strokes and marks made with your brush. Painting your picture is relaxing; you are feeling peaceful and calm. Enjoy creating your artwork. Perhaps you will use all the colours you have selected or maybe you have changed your mind. Whatever you want to create is up to you. There is no right or wrong.

The time has come to finish your picture. Put your brush down and step away from the canvas so you can appreciate your master piece. Wow, what a wonderful creation.

Special Places visualization B2:2

Today you are going to spend some time in a place that is special to you: your very own special place. This is a place you can visit in your imagination when you want to feel safe, powerful and secure. This place can be anywhere you want: somewhere that feels calm and relaxing, a place you already know or somewhere imaginary. It can be an ocean, a desert, an island, a forest, a cave, a castle, on the moon, on a star or in a simple closet under the stairs. It is the first image that comes to you when you hear the words 'special place'.

To get there simply...

Picture a door; this is your special door. Notice what colour it is. Open the door and enter through it; as you do so your special place unfolds in front of your eyes. Take a moment to look around and explore it with your eyes. What do you see around you?

It is so wonderful here. Do you recognize it or is this your first visit? Take a moment to breathe deeply and familiarize yourself with this place. Know that this is your own creation, so if you would like to add anything to it or take something away you can.

Notice whether you are alone or if there are other people here. You can allow anyone in or can ask someone to leave. Only you can decide.

As you move around your special place you feel so happy, so calm, so safe and so confident. This is your special place and it is exactly how you need and want it to be.

Find somewhere to sit or lie down. Maybe it's a comfortable armchair, a large floor cushion, a fluffy cloud or a cosy bed. Once you have found a place, notice how you feel. Breathe deeply and enjoy being still and relaxed in your special place. You can stay here for as long as you like and return here whenever you like; all you have to do is picture your door and step through it into your special place.

For now, however, your visit is coming to an end and you will soon find yourself back where you started.

Dreams visualization B2:3

Picture yourself feeling very tired and very sleepy. It is time to go to sleep and to dream. Feel very light, as if you are floating away to some distant land. You feel very relaxed. You are floating higher and higher into the sky, surrounded by clouds and stars. It is rather magical.

You feel yourself slowing to a halt and are now cushioned on a soft, white cloud. It reminds you of being warm and comfortable in your bed at home, surrounded by your cosy covers and familiar cushions. This cloud is secure.

You notice that all around you are every single one of the dreams you have ever had and are going to have. They pass you like rays of light and you know what each and every one is. Some are good dreams that you have stored away and remember fondly, whilst some are bad dreams that you wish you could forget. Some are bright, reminding you of friends and family and the happy memories you have shared, whilst some are magical and abstract and don't really make sense. Others are dark and quite scary.

Feel within the grip of your palm a dream catcher. What does your dream catcher look like? Does it have a certain shape? Does it have a web or a net? Is it a particular colour? Does it have any decoration or is it plain?

Use your dream catcher to reach out and touch those unhappy dreams that you want to get rid of. Holding it up, you invite your dreams over and one by one, all of the good dreams flow through the catcher and straight into your heart. All the bad ones get tangled within the catcher and can no longer reach you.

If you want to you can add your perfect dream into your dream world. Remember, dreams are very powerful so you can add whatever you wish. The possibilities in your dreams are endless.

Now it is time to leave this soft, white cloud. You begin to float gently back down to the ground. Notice the cool, firm floor beneath your body.

Magic visualization B2:4

Picture yourself at the bottom of a long, winding staircase. Slowly and surely, one step at a time, go up the stairs. Keep going until you reach the top.

Here at the top you discover a door. It looks very old and it is covered with beautifully carved shapes, letters and symbols. Trace your fingers around some of these patterns and then reach out to turn the large, golden doorknob. The door swings open and you find yourself in a wizard's study. Coloured light streams in from the stained glass window and illuminates the room, making it appear magical.

Take a look around. In the corner you see a bookcase filled with dusty old spell books, bottles of all shapes and sizes and jars full of weird and wonderful objects.

In the centre of the room, standing on three iron legs, is a bubbling cauldron. Walk over to it and peer inside. You feel the warmth of the steam and marvel at the colours of the bubbles floating out of the magical liquid. Try popping one; what sound does it make?

You feel like making a spell. Return to the bookcase and select a bottle. Which one have you chosen? What size and shape is it? What sort of stopper does it have? I wonder what your spell will be. Think what it is you would like. Perhaps you need help with something, or there's something you've always wanted.

It is time to collect all your ingredients – feathers, stars, whatever you need; they are in named jars on the third shelf of the bookcase. Place all your ingredients into the liquid inside the cauldron and mix really well with the wooden spoon. What colour is your potion? Is it bubbling or steaming? Now say your spell. A spell is like a wish and can be anything you want.

Carefully pour your mixture into the bottle you have chosen. Ensure you have put the lid on and pop the potion bottle into your pocket.

Suddenly, the clock on the wall chimes three times. It is time to leave before the wizard returns! Go back to the door, twist the large, golden doorknob once more and make your way back down the stairs.

Characters visualization B2:5

Picture yourself sitting in a very large, very comfortable and very cosy chair. Settle down, take a few deep breaths and enjoy feeling relaxed and calm.

Notice a colourful comic book on your lap. Reading the title, you notice that a word is missing. It simply says 'The Adventures of…' Confused, you flick through the pages and see that they are blank. Suddenly, letters begin to appear on the front cover completing the comic's title and, to your amazement, they spell out your name!

Excitedly, you flick through the pages once more only to discover that the pages are now filled with words and pictures.

You notice that there is only one character throughout the whole book. Picture this character in your mind. Study them carefully; try to recognize the part they are playing. What are they wearing? What are they doing? What stories are they a part of? Do you recognize this character or is this the first time you have seen them? The drawings and stories of this character fascinate you.

Continue turning the pages. Look closely at the character's face and try to recognize the emotion they are showing. Their expression is different on each page. Sometimes they appear happy, sad, afraid or excited. On occasion, it is difficult to recognize how they are feeling but they are feeling it nevertheless and are pleased that you have noticed. What would you say to this character if you could? Send them a message in your mind.

It is time to close the comic book now and say goodbye to this character. As you put the book away, think about what adventures they have had. I wonder what will happen to them next. Perhaps next time you'll find out.

Animals visualization B3:1

Picture yourself on a bright, sunny day. On the ground in front of you is a smooth, circular space. Watch carefully as an animal begins to appear; slowly at first, and it may be difficult to make out. Don't worry if you cannot see it clearly yet; it will make itself fully known to you as soon as it is ready. Keep watching.

This is your special animal. It has a connection to you. Observe it carefully. How big or small is it? Does it have fur? Feathers? Does it have scales or something altogether different? What colour is the animal? Does it have any special markings or patterns on its face and body?

How does your animal move? Does it move slowly and gracefully or quickly and clumsily? Maybe it doesn't walk at all, maybe it glides and swoops through the air or bobs and swishes through the ocean. You decide. This is your special animal.

Your animal opens its mouth. Listen carefully to hear the sound it makes. Remember there is no right and no wrong; the sound is what you hear it to be and so may not be the sound you expect.

Your animal wants you to discover more about it. It wants to show you where it lives. Go with it to that place and take a look around. You feel privileged that your animal has brought you here; it trusts you and feels comfortable in your company. It likes that you have taken the time to discover more about it.

Time ticks away and day begins to turn to night. You need to return to your own home. Before you go, your special animal presents you with a gift. What has it given you? Perhaps it has given you one of its skills or talents, or one of the qualities that makes it special? It wants you to feel special, and you do.

As you leave, wave goodbye to your animal and watch as it ever so slowly fades away. It is gone now, but you have the gift it has given you and the memory of it, forever.

Deep Space visualization B3:2

Picture yourself journeying into space. You are gently floating up into the sky; it feels wonderful to fly. You feel safe and secure as you rise higher and higher. Feel the soft, cooling air against your face. It is completely silent and you feel calm and confident.

Take time to explore the wondrous sights in space. Look around. You are amazed by what you see. There are twinkling stars glistening all around you. What a magical place to be! You reach out with your hand to touch one. Feel the weight of it in your palm and gaze at its silver glow.

In front of you, a shooting star dashes by. Hear the whoosh as it rushes past.

In the distance, the moon is beaming boldly. If you look closely you can see it is not smooth but dotted with large dips and holes.

The planets are vast and each surface is covered with different colours, mesmerizing swirls and glorious patterns. Enjoy gliding through this immense space that is full of such colours and sights.

You approach the sun and, as you pass, feel the wonderful warmth on your face, your arms, your legs and your body.

Your eyes search past the stars, sun and moon. What else can you see in the sky? This is your very own universe. What exists here? Are there comets or black holes, or perhaps an entirely new planet or galaxies with worlds of their own? If you want to you can invite anyone you please into your universe. Take a few moments to appreciate and enjoy this magnificent scene.

It is time to leave this space. What an adventure! If you like it, you can keep the memory of what you have seen. As you breathe in you feel so content and drift back gently towards the Earth.

Weather visualization B3:3

Picture yourself in the doorway of a small tent. In the centre of the tent is a table that is close to the ground, low enough to sit next to and covered with a purple, silk cloth. On the table is a mysterious object. It is not clear what this is yet but you will see very soon. Looking around the table, picture large, comfortable cushions scattered on the floor.

Follow the path towards the centre table and choose a cushion to sit down on. The mysterious object is a round crystal ball. It is quite beautiful, but it is empty. You reach out and slide your palm down one side of it to feel how perfectly smooth it is.

With another touch, a whirlwind fills the once clear and still crystal ball. Within a mere second you are staring at an enchanting snow scene. Glinting snowflakes fall silently and elegantly to the white, snow blanket covering the floor. Tree tops are smothered in the settling snow, like a sprinkling of icing on a cake. Delicate footprints create paths between the forest trees but no animals can be seen. What a beautiful and peaceful sight. Notice how this makes you feel.

Touch the glass again and watch the whirlwind change the scene. This time, there are lush, green, open fields. Dry, unmarked, country roads separate the fields and wooden fences frame the edges. The sky is grey and gloomy; the clouds threaten to burst with rain. Gusts of wind whip up leaves and loose strings of hay. A funnel shape soon develops in the centre of the crystal, the clouds swirl and a tornado appears. It is very powerful. Notice how this makes you feel.

You touch the glass for a final time and the whirlwind evaporates, revealing a glorious, bright day. The sky is as blue as can be, with not a single cloud visible. The sun beams boldly over a sandy beach and you can feel the warmth escaping the crystal ball. The sea is calm and dazzling in the sunlight. Notice how this makes you feel.

It is time to leave the tent and this enchanting crystal ball. You can revisit another time if you wish. Before you leave cover the ball with the purple cloth next to you. It is very safe here.

Secret Garden visualization B3:4

Picture yourself before a large wooden door, covered with ivy and vines. It is a very curious door and you'd like to know what is behind it. You notice a keyhole and peer through it. Through this door is your very own secret garden that you are going to create. It isn't like anyone else's and no one has ever seen it before. It is somewhere you can go to relax and take some time out.

Notice a door handle in the centre of the door. Excitedly, you reach out to turn it and pass through the doorway. You feel relieved and relaxed to be inside your secret garden.

Feel the ground underneath your toes. Are you standing on freshly cut grass or a cool, stony pathway? You notice a stone tablet on the wall next to you; it says 'Welcome to your secret garden.'

There is a wall surrounding the garden. It is peaceful and safe here. Explore your garden. Use all your senses to take in your surroundings. You take a deep breath and enjoy feeling so relaxed. Are there colourful flowers and plants? Can you hear water? Perhaps you see a river trickling between gravelled pathways or a fountain splashing playfully against the rocks. Perhaps butterflies are dancing upon the branches or birds are swooping between the trees. Enjoy looking at all the wonderful things in your garden.

Notice a fresh patch of soil and sit next to it. This patch of earth is ready for planting. Perhaps you would like to plant something here. Is there a memory or feeling or even something special you would like to store in your secret garden? The garden will keep it very safe for you. Or perhaps there is something you want to change. You can plant it here in your garden and, like a seed, it will transform and grow into something beautiful. Take a moment to plant anything that you want to at this time. Remember to pat the earth down so that the garden can nurture it. Now, just like your surroundings, you feel peaceful and calm.

It is time to leave your garden. Remember you can return whenever you want. Head towards the door and, with a last look, take a deep breath and lock the door behind you.

Mirrors and Masks visualization B3:5

Picture yourself in front of a marbled mantelpiece upon which sits a large mirror. What sort of mirror do you see? What shape is it? Is the edge ornate and bejewelled or old, simple and plain? Take some time to scan the frame of your mirror so you can see it clearly.

Look in the mirror; can you read your expression? Are you smiling and relaxed? Or is your reflection showing something different? Whatever you are seeing, try to understand the emotion on your face; this may be difficult, so don't worry if you can't.

Notice that in front of the mirror there are three blank, white masks. In a moment you are going to choose what these faces will look like. What do you want them to be? What emotions will they show?

Now take some time to think of three feelings that come to your mind. Perhaps you felt one today. Perhaps it is something you feel often. Or maybe it is a feeling that you don't like but sometimes feel. Choose the first three that pop into your head, each one appearing on a mask. If you find it difficult to imagine the emotions, you can simply decorate the masks with anything you want.

Starting with your first mask, place it carefully on your face and gaze at yourself in the mirror. Remember you can take your mask off at any time. What do you see staring back at you? Take a moment to absorb the mask. What does it make you feel inside?

When you are ready, switch to your second mask. Again, observe the reflection that you see and take a moment to see what it makes you feel. Does this mask feel different?

Finally, when you are ready, put on your final mask. Does this feel comfortable? Does this feel any different? Which one was your favourite? Or did you not like any?

It is now time to take off the third mask, replacing all three on the mantelpiece. You are pleased to be seeing your own reflection again! When you are ready, turn away from the mirror.

Circus visualization B4:1

Picture yourself at an opening in a striped wall. The wall is flexible to touch and moves as you press your palm against it. This is the wall of a large circus tent; the opening is the entrance. Your ears pick up the sound of fun, laughter and joy from inside the tent. Step inside and discover the circus for yourself.

Travel down the corridor. At the end is a lady who welcomes and gestures you to step through a curtain. You do so happily and, to your excitement, see that you are standing in the circus ring; take a seat and settle down to watch the show.

The ringmaster appears and the crowd grows silent. With a huge round of applause, the acrobats are introduced. They burst into the arena and come cartwheeling in with sequined costumes that glitter and glint under the parade of spotlights. They glide and swoop so effortlessly on the high trapeze; it amazes you. Silently they swing, back and forth, making fantastical twists, turns and somersaults.

Below them a troop of jugglers appear with bright red noses and playful outfits. Skilfully, they cast brightly coloured balls, flaming torches and fragile china plates into the air. Astonishingly, not one item falls to the ground. The crowd are on the edge of their seats watching the jugglers, willing them to succeed.

Slowly, the atmosphere changes, the show lights dim, the sounds from the crowd die down and one bright spotlight focuses on the centre of the ring. A new, never-before-seen act emerges from the shadows. What do you see? Is it a single performer or a group working together. Notice how the crowd reacts around you and how you feel about what you are seeing. As you continue to watch, is there anything that stands out to you? Are you surprised by what you see or impressed by their talent? Perhaps you were hoping to see something different. For now, you experience this spectacle with your fellow audience.

It is time for the show to end. The lights begin to glow a little brighter and the crowd disperses. You make your way to the exit, passing the smiling lady once more. As you leave, you wonder – what kind of circus act would you be?

Deserts visualization B4:2

Picture yourself at the top of a hill of sand. Above you is a clear, blue sky and a sun that showers you with warmth and comfort. Feel the soft sand beneath your feet and enjoy this feeling of calm.

You are on a sand dune. It is the tallest dune in the desert and from here you can see into the far distance. The desert appears to sweep on forever. You can see no beginning and no end to it. It seems as though the desert is completely empty except for the sand dunes that roll across the landscape. It is as if you are looking at a never-ending sea of soft, sandy waves.

It is so peaceful here. You imagine that you might be the only person in the entire world and that feels ok. You settle yourself down to sit in the sand and notice how it warmly hugs your body in a secure embrace. From here you can watch the desert more closely and, as you do so, you notice that there is more to it than you originally thought.

Look carefully now and pick out all the things that you hadn't noticed before. Perhaps you see a lone rock or twisted tree. Maybe a tiny colourful lizard scurrying by or snake basking in the hot desert sun. You may even see water; a tiny oasis perhaps with a palm tree and a spring. Even the grains of sand are not as they first appeared. You notice that each one is slightly different in size, in shape and in colour. Run your fingers through the sand and marvel at how, when combined, the grains form the softest, dreamiest desert sand.

The desert is so much more than you ever imagined it to be and you continue to explore it with your eyes as you relax on your spot on the tallest sand dune until it is time to leave. Until the air grows cooler, the light begins to fade and the hot desert sun disappears on the horizon.

Hats and Headdresses visualization B4:3

Picture yourself in front of a large door. Turn the handle and, as you step through, hear the bell that rings each time the door is open. You recognize that you are in a shop – a shop filled with all kinds of interesting and unusual hats and headdresses. Take a moment to scan the room and see which ones catch your eye.

As you look around, a friendly shop assistant appears and ushers you to follow them through to a room at the back of the store. You do so happily and discover that you have been led to a small, mirrored room with a table. On the table, a number of hats and headdresses have been carefully laid out. The shop assistant draws a curtain behind you and leaves you to try some of them on for yourself.

Pick up the first hat or headdress from the table. What kind is it? Notice the shape and the colour. What sort of person would be likely to wear it? As you place it on your head, look into the mirror and feel a transformation taking place within you. Notice how it makes you feel.

Now take the hat or headdress off and try on another from the table. This one looks very different from the last one, but once again it makes you feel transformed. You may try on as many as you wish. Simply place them back onto the table when you have finished.

It is time to pull the curtain back across now. The shop assistant is waiting for you and says that, if you would like to, you are welcome to take either a hat or a headdress with you. They advise you to take one that you feel best expresses who you are or who you would like to be. Gratefully, you choose one. You bid the assistant farewell and head back out through the shop. Turn the handle of the door once more, step out and don't forget to listen out for the bell as you leave.

Pockets visualization B4:4

Picture yourself sitting comfortably on a cosy, cushioned chair. In front of you is a selection of fabrics in all different colours and patterns and a huge selection of decorations; perhaps some buttons, shapes or jewels. These craft materials are here to help you make your very own pocket.

Take a moment to select the fabric you want to make your pocket with. Think about the size and shape of your pocket. You may be drawn to a particular type of fabric. Perhaps it will be a silk pocket or maybe a velvet one. What colour is this fabric? Perhaps it is many colours or just one. Handle the fabric of your pocket carefully, cut out the shape and sew the sides using a needle and thread. The more time you spend on creating your special pocket, the better it will be.

Once you have sewn your pocket, you may like to add some decorations or details; choose from your imagination. Perhaps there are threads, beads, sparkly sequins or something entirely different. Or maybe your pocket doesn't need any decoration. Once you have finished your pocket, enjoy looking at what you have created.

Take some time to think about things that are important to you that you would like to keep in this pocket. It may be a particular object or perhaps a memory or feeling; it could even be someone special to you. Only you know what is in this pocket. You can remove it at any time; until then be confident that it is safe and secure.

Finally, it is time to close your pocket up; you may like to fasten a button or zip to it or leave it exactly how it is. Now that you have this pocket, you can use it whenever you wish. Just close your eyes and it will appear.

Footprints visualization B4:5

Picture yourself alone on a sandy beach. It is a summer's day. Take a moment to look around you and take in the peaceful surroundings. Perhaps it is a beautiful, bright day with blue skies and calm waves, or maybe it is dusk and the sun is setting on the horizon; the choice is yours.

As you move along the shore, look down at your feet – you have no shoes on; feel the wet surface between your bare toes. With each step your foot sinks gently into the ground. As you continue to stroll along the shore, notice that many footprints are being created in the sand. The texture of the sand feels smooth and soft, and it cushions the soles of your feet. Take a deep breath and continue to create your footprints along the sand; with each step, a footprint appears behind you. Look carefully at the footprints you have already made. Are they flat or have they actually pressed themselves into the floor? What colour are they? Perhaps they are in many colours or just one. Crouch down and trace the shape of your footprint with your finger. Is there something you would like to change about your footprints – the size or maybe even the direction? Does your path of footprints stretch out for miles or are there only a few?

Continue to tread along the trail you are creating. You now notice something surprising in front of you. There are not only footprints behind you, but they are in front of you as well. It's as if they are mapping your journey ahead of you. How many sets of pathways can you see? Is there one, two or many? It is up to you whether you want to continue on this path or whether you are curious about another; you can go in any direction you wish.

Perhaps you would like to explore them now or another time when you revisit them? It seems there is always an option when you are making a choice. As you look back, can you still see your footprints or are they no longer there? Your journey is completely unique to you.

Books visualization B5:1

Picture yourself in a great library lined with many wooden bookcases. You find yourself before one of them; the most important one in the library. On one of the shelves is a very special book waiting to be found. Search the titles until you find it and then take it down from the shelf.

Run your fingers along the spine, taking in the weight, texture and general appearance of the book. Is it large or small? Does it contain many pages or just a few? Notice the cover now. Are there any pictures or words? Try to see it clearly in your mind. There is no other book like it; it is actually a book all about you. Within its pages are the stories that have happened in your life so far. There is nothing frightening in this book because everything in it has already been and is in the past. Nothing in the book can hurt you.

Open the book and turn to the first page. This is the contents page and on here you find a list of all the chapters in the book so far. Is there a chapter for every year of your life? Or perhaps it is simply a list of life memories and moments. Maybe there is a page for every day or for every hour. You decide; you know best; this is your book.

Choose a title from the list, find the page number and turn to it. Spend some time now looking at that page. Is it just writing or are there pictures too? You can read the page if you like or turn to another. The choice is yours and you are welcome to look at as many pages as you would like.

The caretaker arrives and rattles a bunch of keys to let you know that the library will be closing shortly. Close the book and place it safely back on the shelf where you found it. Here it will stay until you choose to look at it again.

Hot Air Balloons visualization B5:2

Picture a large, open field. The sun is beaming brightly, there isn't a single cloud in the sky and the breeze is calm and cool.

Notice that there are hot air balloons dotted in the field as far as your eyes can see. It is a wonderful sight. Each one has a wooden wicker basket to hold its passengers and a colourful, vibrant balloon. Some are plain colours; others have multi-coloured stripes and patterns decorating them. All the balloons are inflated with a powerful flame that swooshes heat up into the air now and again. The strong puffing flame creates an impressive sound that whooshes past your eyes. Begin to walk through the forest of the hot air balloons. Take in the colours and listen to the flames.

It's time to enjoy a ride in one of these balloons. Select one that you are drawn to. Notice what your balloon looks like and climb into the secure, strong basket. As you get in look up to see the fire fill the balloon with hot air; feel the warmth that radiates off the flames. The balloon is very safe and will glide smoothly through the sky. The ropes holding your basket down are released slowly and carefully. Take a deep breath and feel the balloon gracefully lift off the ground. You are floating higher and higher.

As you climb upwards, notice your surroundings: the view is incredible but completely unique to you; this is your journey. What can you see? Perhaps there are lush forests, vast oceans or something entirely different. This is a very special journey because you can choose exactly where you would like to go. Is there somewhere you have always dreamed of visiting? Or someplace that you are familiar with that you would like to go to now? Perhaps your flight will take you to someone you have been hoping or wishing to see? Take a few moments to think about the possibilities. You are in control of your destination; simply release the flame and gently drift away. I wonder where your journey will take you.

Textures visualization B5:3

Picture yourself snuggled up on a sofa. On your lap is a large, colourful blanket made from many squares of fabric, all neatly sewed together. This is a patchwork blanket and each square looks and feels different to the next.

Run your hands over the blanket and notice how each square patch feels different against your skin. Some are silky and smooth; others are rough and scratchy; some are tickly and feel unusual. There are patches that feel hard and soft, cool and warm. Scaly patches, bouncy patches, crinkly patches, patches of every kind of texture imaginable. See how many different textures you can feel and try and name them in your mind.

Find a square patch on the blanket that feels enjoyable to touch. Concentrate on that patch now; explore it with the palm of your hand and the tips of your fingers. How does the patch feel? How does it make you feel? Does it remind you of anything? What does it make you think about?

Now try to find a square patch on the blanket that feels unusual to touch. It might be strange because it is an unfamiliar texture: surprising, uncomfortable or peculiar. Like before, concentrate on that patch now; once again, feel it with the palm of your hand and the tips of your fingers. How does the patch feel? How does it make you feel? Does it remind you of anything? What does it make you think about?

If you could choose the squares on your very own patchwork blanket, which textures would you choose? How would you want each patch to make you feel? Take some time to create it in your mind. Choose as many textures as you like and combine them to create your blanket.

Wrap this new blanket around you and enjoy how it makes you feel.

Messages visualization B5:4

Picture yourself sitting comfortably on a chair at a desk. This is where you will write or draw some important messages. Take a moment to look at what items are on your desk; there may be some flowers, a special pencil case, a pile of books – you decide. Notice that there is a notebook with your name written on the front and a pen of your choice next to it. What does this look like?

To begin with, you are going to learn how to get rid of negative messages that may be in your mind. These could be any thoughts or feelings that you would like to let go of. Perhaps there are some worries, concerns, conversations or situations. Or maybe there is something that has made you feel sad, angry or anxious. Now open your notebook to the first page and, using your pen, jot them down. You may need to use more than one page; it's up to you. Notice how you feel as you do so. When you have finished, tear the paper out of your notebook. Use all your energy to scrunch the paper up. Feel the weight of those negative thoughts lifted from your mind and the sense of relief as you crush them.

Then throw these pages away. Take a deep breath; you have now let go of those negative messages.

You feel calm and content. There is a fresh piece of paper in front of you. It is time to fill your notebook with positive messages. These could be drawings, words, stories or thoughts. Perhaps there is something in particular you often forget to tell yourself or something you need to remind yourself of in order to feel more confident and relaxed. Perhaps you need to remember the wonderful qualities you already have.

When you have completed your writing or drawing, close your notebook. How does it feel to know the pages of your notebook are now full of wonderfully positive messages? Remember to read over them often and add to them any time you wish.

Butterflies visualization B5:5

Picture yourself curled up in a warm, cosy space. All around you is the dim glow of a single colour. It feels as though you are wonderfully wrapped up, as if you are tucked in a perfectly safe and secure blanket. Enjoy the feeling of being snuggled up here.

As you lie there, you begin to feel as if you want to break free from this confined place; you feel the need to stretch your arms and legs and move freely. It is important to know that before you go you can leave behind any unwanted thoughts or feelings. Whatever you leave in this space you can let go of for good. Perhaps there is a negative feeling, something that makes you feel sad, angry or anxious. Maybe it is a memory or someone in particular that you do not wish to keep with you. Allow those thoughts to spill out into this cocoon.

It is time to push your way out. Use your strength to reach your arms above your head and force your hands through the surface layer. Feel the cool air outside as your fingers break free. Use this opening to slowly create a bigger hole in your cocoon. The sides break down with ease and little effort. You are excited to fly outside with a fresh mind. You feel light and eager to see what is in store now that all the negativity is behind you.

You notice something magical has happened as you emerge. You realize you have beautiful, strong wings attached to your shoulders. What colour are your wings? Perhaps they are bright and bold or pale and twinkle in the light. Take them in.

When you're ready, take a step forward and look at your surroundings. As you step forward, feel your wings flutter to help you balance. You are eager to fly and see what is in store. Feel your confidence rise as you prepare to launch; remember that you can rely on your wings to carry you. You are totally safe… get ready, take a deep breath and in… 3, 2, 1… fly. Enjoy the feeling of soaring through the sky and the total freedom.

Rocks visualization B6:1

Picture a cave. It is dark but light enough for you to see, as natural light streams in from little cracks in the rock ceiling above your head. The walls are made from smooth stone and are cold to touch. The cave is an empty place. It would make a good shelter from the wind and harsh weather outside but you have not come here to find shelter. You have come here to discover a very special kind of rock.

This rock is hidden deep within the cave, so first you must reach into your pocket and take out the handy torch that you had forgotten you kept there. You will be venturing down into the cave and the natural light that floods in where you are standing now will not be there when you reach the special rock.

If you haven't already done so, switch on the torch and head towards the darkest part of the cave. The ground is firm beneath your feet and the stone walls either side of you are strong and secure. Keep walking and enjoy the silence that exists here. You feel calm and know that you will soon make your discovery.

As you near the end of the cave, the light from your torch picks out a small doorway. It is a natural doorway that nature has carved into the rock. Pass through it now and find yourself in a stone chamber. In the centre of this chamber is a very special rock. It is your rock; there is no rock like it anywhere else in the world. Walk towards it and shine your torch brightly so you can take in the details of this rock. Notice its size, its shape and its colour. Run your hands over it and feel its texture and temperature.

This rock is special. To others it may seem to be just a rock but you know different. This rock has true worth, simply for being the rock that it is. Carefully pick it up and place it in your pocket; you have made your discovery. Pass back through the doorway now and make your way towards the light. The rock is yours now and will remind you that, like it, you are special.

Jellyfish Flurry visualization B6:2

Picture yourself gently floating under the surface of the cool, calm sea. The water is bright and warm; you can see the light streaming through the bobbing waves above. Take a moment to look around; you are not by yourself – you are amongst a flurry of other jellyfish. These jellyfish are welcoming and friendly and you feel comfortable and happy to be with them.

As you take in what you can see, enjoy being swept softly through the water with the light water current; it feels wonderful to be swaying in the ocean with the other jellyfish.

Take a closer look at the jellyfish around you. What do they look like? Are they different sizes? Are they one colour or multi-coloured? What expressions can you see on their faces? How do you feel being amongst these jellyfish?

Do some of them know each other? I wonder what they are saying to one another? As you look around, focus on one jellyfish that stands out and you are drawn to. Swim over to that particular jellyfish. As you approach, the jellyfish turns towards you and smiles. They are delighted you have come to meet them. Perhaps you would like to talk to them; what would you like to say to this jellyfish? Take some time to talk and listen.

Perhaps another jellyfish joins you or you want to introduce yourself to them.

It is now time to leave your jellyfish flurry and say goodbye to some of them, but remember you can always come back to visit them any time you like. As you wave goodbye, turn away from the fading flurry and head back to the surface.

Puppets visualization B6:3

Picture a slumped, lifeless puppet. The puppet has strings attached to the top of its head, arms and legs, and they are all fastened to wooden handles. This is a very special puppet because it belongs to you. It can be exactly what and who you want it to be.

Pick up the handles of your puppet. It instantly jumps up and patiently waits to be brought to life. Focus on the blank face in front of you. What expression can you see? What hair and eyes does your puppet have? Begin to design what your puppet is wearing and what it looks like in your mind. Perhaps it looks like someone you know or is completely different to what you expected to see.

Now think about the character of your puppet: what qualities would you like it to have? Is it confident or shy? Is it happy or sad? Does it have any special gifts? Perhaps you would like to give it a name.

Use the handles to encourage your puppet to move. Raise the strings so that the arms lift and then practise gently pulling the strings connected to the legs.

Next to your puppet is a handmade, mini stage. Choose whatever backdrop and props you would like for your puppet. Perhaps you want to create somewhere you know or somewhere new, somewhere real or imaginary. Place your puppet on the stage and use the handles to pull the strings. Enjoy watching as it performs and expresses itself freely.

It is time for your puppet to sleep, but remember you can use your puppet again whenever you like.

Angels visualization B6:4

Picture yourself in a white space; it is not a room or somewhere you recognize, it is just the colour white, speckled with bursts of light. You feel relaxed and curious. You cannot feel the floor below your feet; notice that you are hovering in this special space – you feel weightless.

It is time to discover more about this extraordinary place. Focus on one of the bursts of light and notice now how it gently glows, it slowly pulses in and out of view and it radiates with warmth and wonder. The longer you stare at this light, the clearer it becomes; you are drawn towards the light as it grows larger and brighter. The clear, white light begins to take a shape as it draws nearer; feel the sense of peace as this heavenly being reaches you.

With absolute amazement and awe you realize that you are in the presence of an angel. Your own angel. The angel welcomes you with open arms and a pure heart. With your eyes, take a few moments to scan them. How are their wings shaped? Do they have a face? What are they wearing?

Your angel understands and knows you very well already; it has been protecting you and listening to you since your first days in the world. Feel how safe and calm you feel in its presence. Perhaps you would like to talk to your angel. You can speak to it at any time. Your angel is here to support and guide you; you can revisit it whenever you want to. It is always with you, although you may not always see it.

Your angel now begins to fade; once a bright, clear shape, the edges of your angel now begin to blur. Watch as your angel slowly returns to a glowing light once again. It has gone to join other angels and return to its duty of watching over you.

Inventions visualization B6:5

Picture yourself next to a tall table. This is not just any table; this is a workbench and on it you will be able to make your very own invention. You are an inventor and this is the special place where you can create all the things that you need to make your life easier, happier and healthier.

Let's invent something now. What is it that you would like to invent? This could be anything you like so long as it is not an invention that could be used to harm yourself, others or any other living creature. Think carefully as to what might help to make you feel even better about yourself. Is there something that could help you to feel more confident, more calm or more happy? Perhaps it will be an invention that could help you to do something more easily or safely remove something that is not especially helpful to you right now.

Maybe you have an idea now, but don't worry if you don't. Once you start creating on your workbench, your invention, whatever it may be, will come to light.

All around you are the materials you need to make your invention. Whatever you need, it is here; simply collect the things you need. Don't forget any helpful tools; they are all here too. You just need to think of them and, as if by magic, they will appear.

See yourself putting together all the materials you have collected. You do this confidently because you are an inventor. Keep going until you have finished your invention.

You've done it. You are a truly talented inventor. You now know that on your workbench you can bring together all the things that you need to help you be the person you want to be and feel the way that you want to feel. Well done you.

Glossary

Art resource station The area where all the art and craft materials used for creative expression are set out

Block A group of five Jellyfish classes

Bodywork Poses, stretches and movements

Brushing off An action used in the initial gathering

Creative chatter A conversation about what has been created

Creative expression Responding to a theme using art and craft materials

Exploring the theme Activities used in the class to inspire creative expression

Final gathering Coming together at the end of a class to share and appreciate creative expression

Focus point The centre of the gathering place

Gathering place The area around the focus point

Initial gathering The start of the class

Jellyfish breathing A breathing sequence used at the start of the class

Jellyfish cards Cards that depict a jellyfish displaying an emotion or feeling

Jellyfish gift cards Word cards given as a gift at the end of each class

Jellyfish motto There is no right or wrong

Jellyfish strands Underpin each Jellyfish class and are linked to our aims

Jellyfish teacher The adult/s delivering a Jellyfish class

Jellyfish wave A technique used to send positive intentions and ideas

On the shore Questions to open creative chatter conversation

Personal signature A symbol used to signify the end of massage

Sensory and relaxation zone A space intended for quiet and used for relaxing, exploring and time out

Task An activity used to explore a theme

Under the sea Questions to develop creative chatter discussion

Visualization A story read to encourage imagination and calm